A New Story of Wholeness

An Experiential Guide
for Connecting the Human Family

A New Story of Wholeness

An Experiential Guide
for Connecting the Human Family

Robert Atkinson

Light on Light press

Books may be purchased through booksellers or by contacting Sacred Stories Publishing.

Cover Holos design by Brian Berman holosamulets.com

A New Story of Wholeness
An Experiential Guide for Connecting the Human Family
Robert Atkinson

Tradepaper ISBN: 978-1-958921-09-8
EBook ISBN: 978-1-958921-10-4

Library of Congress Control Number: 2022945445

Published by Light on Light Press
An imprint of Sacred Stories Publishing, Fort Lauderdale, FL

Printed in the United States of America

Advance Praise
A New Story of Wholeness

In *A New Story of Wholeness* Dr. Robert Atkinson invites us to remember the fundamental unity of which we are all-ways part and at the deepest levels of our awareness, already know. Inspirationally and compassionately he masterfully co-weaves unitive narratives from mythology, mysticism, ritual, and psychology to reveal the same universal patterns of evolutionary consciousness. His wonder-full synthesis and experiential and eminently practical wisdom is a marvellously valuable companion and guide for these transformational and emergent times, along, as he describes 'an interspiritual path that is a superhighway for everyone' on our collective journey of homecoming.

– **Jude Currivan** PhD, cosmologist, co-founder Whole World-View, and author of *The Cosmic Hologram* and *The Story of GAIA*

A New Story of Wholeness asserts itself among the great texts on spiritual evolution and Unity consciousness. Filled with mystical yet practical wisdom, it offers guidance and tools for our transformational journey back to our awareness of our innate divinity and Oneness, allowing us to create and share a new narrative for ourselves, as well as humanity, grounded in love, harmony, and interconnection. Study this guide. Your new life awaits you.

– **Michael Bernard Beckwith**, founder & CEO, Agape International Spiritual Center and author of *Life Visioning*

A New Story of Wholeness is a gem offering superbly lucid and wise guidance for the journey from fragmentation to optimal coherence and richly fulfilling wholeness. It is a journey that we all must take if we are to thrive in dangerous times.

– **James O'Dea**, author of *Cultivating Peace*, *The Conscious Activist*, and *Soul Awakening Practice*

With this heartfelt, wise book, Bob Atkinson invites us to take a joyful journey into wholeness – beyond boundaries that we hold within ourselves and others – to emerge as full social artists. Through sharing the wisdom of indigenous and modern scientific perspectives on human evolution and interconnection, as well as his own practical guidance for personal transformation, Atkinson's writings will delight and inspire you to co-create the world we know is possible.

– **Shamini Jain**, PhD, founder & CEO, Consciousness and Healing Initiative and author of *Healing Ourselves*

What a gift! *A New Story of Wholeness* is a brilliant synthesis of the psycho-spiritual pilgrimage, developmental process, and evolutionary trajectory of wholeness. Each page is sprinkled with wisdom and inspiration that supports the expansion of consciousness. It holds such a beautiful energetic resonance that even the space between the lines seem to answer the age-old questions of where we came from, who we are, and where we're going. There's a perfect blend of art, science, and the intimate inter-spiritual path. Not only will it inspire a shift toward a *whole* worldview, but it also encourages each of us to live for the *good of the whole*. This important guidebook is everything humanity needs, individually and collectively, to recognize our inherent wholeness, evolve and transform the world.

> – **Julie Krull,** award winning author of *Fractured Grace* and host of the Dr. Julie Show: All Things Connected

Our default setting is to divide, separate, and cordon off; to perceive the world and the beings that inhabit it in parts, pieces, and fragments. In this concise, eloquent book, Robert Atkinson points the way to a desperately needed upgrade: to wholeness, fullness, and connection. This is a journey, but the path is well-trod, the guideposts are in place, and the way forward could not be more fulfilling—or more urgent. Our future depends on our willingness to heed Atkinson's call.

> – **Philip Goldberg**, author of *American Veda* and *Spiritual Practice for Crazy Times*

Written with great love, this gentle excursion into the sacred emphasizes what all spiritual teachings express — that higher consciousness brings a realization of unity that can heal our world. Addressing the need for a new myth to guide us into the future, this work combines the best wisdom of many esteemed leaders and teachers. It takes you through the stages of initiation and gives you a practical way to bring theory into practice through reflective writing exercises. A true manifesto for the spiritual awakening so needed in these times.

– **Anodea Judith** PhD, author of *The Global Heart Awakens; Eastern Body, Western Mind;* and *Wheels of Life*

Most of the challenges and chaos experienced on Earth today result from unconscious living. Imagine a world with only conscious living and conscious storytelling. This is exactly what *A New Story of Wholeness* offers readers – a guide to evolving our consciousness to its fullest potential. This much-needed book is a gift to each of us and to humanity as a whole. We at Humanity's Team encourage everyone to take to heart this book's message, integrate it into your very being, as this book will surely assist the global effort to awaken to the interconnectedness – or Oneness – of everything in the universe!

– **Steve Farrell**, co-founder and worldwide executive director of Humanity's Team

A New Story of Wholeness should be required reading for anyone who wants to know how they can contribute to healing the divides we face personally and collectively. Readers are gently nudged to consider new ways of relating to others and reality through an unfolding process of inquiry, contemplation, and reflection which culminates in the creation of a new narrative of wholeness, hope, and a unified destiny for humanity.

– **Lisa Engles Witter**, psycho-spiritual counselor and coach, meditation teacher, and author

Robert Atkinson's book is a most timely and welcome gift reminding us that we are participants in the never-ending Story of Creation as actors and co-writers. This elegantly crafted offering reveals the plot: namely, that in order to know Itself, the One fractured into a billion pieces and set in motion the journey of the prodigal son and daughter who are called home into Wholeness. Dr Atkinson's invitation at this present time of darkness and division in the world is for us to remember our Oneness with all of Life and to piece together the fractured body of humanity through all that we think, say and do. The underlying message of hope conveyed in this book is that evolution is a progressive entry into greater states of wholeness and awareness.

– **Michael Lindfield**, board president, Meditation Mount, Ojai, California

For civilization to evolve, a new societal story is needed, and this book provides a narrative process that will guide us there. By expanding our worldview, Robert Atkinson transforms our perception of interconnectedness and oneness. An eloquent writer and storyteller, Atkinson offers us creative and practical methods to heal, grow, and step into our individual and collective wholeness. Within these pages is a map for transcendence.

– **Lisa Worth Huber**, PhD, president, National Peace Academy, consultant, educator, and social justice advocate

Contents

Foreword

Reweaving Our Stories

—Jean Houston, PhD

In this time of whole-system transition, we can no longer afford to live as half-light versions of ourselves. Current complexities call for greater and wiser use of our capacities, a more attuned ·playing of the instrument we have been given.

We can now glimpse the possibility of a planetary society heralding the end of ancient enmities and the birth of new ways of using our common humanity and its various cultures. Worldwide, societies are crying for help with the needed transformation of organizations and institutions. We need new ways of looking at and relating to each other, new methods of supporting each other in serving humanity.

The world can thrive only if we can grow. We can only create this possible society if people learn to be the possible humans we are meant to be. We need the potential of the whole human race—and the particular genius of every culture—if we are going to survive our time.

In the new world just ahead, all things will be understood as interconnected. Our ability to dream each other's dreams and experience each other's biographies will be part of this interpenetrating wave of our common memory. We are being rescaled to planetary proportions as we become resonant and intimate with our own depths.

This social evolution requires more social artists, those who bring fresh vision to the community, who seek to transform all levels of society, who are contemplative creators, acting in both silence and service, helping people ignite their potential.

Social artists are those who recognize this interconnectedness and give voice or creative expression to its presence amongst us all. These social artists, especially those conscious storytellers Robert Atkinson speaks of in his introduction to this vital book, are needed to bridge the unknown abyss that separates a dying era from one being born.

Creative social artistry is contemplative, synergizing inner and outer realities necessary for transformation on all levels. This process assists visionary endeavors, unleashes the human spirit, and gives us access to remarkable world-making patterns. Beneath the surface of consciousness, in all of us, creative ideas and solutions are always waiting, ready to bloom into consciousness.

In a world ripe for healing, social artists are the healers of society. They don't seek to fix the old Adam, but to understand the whole Adam. They are motivated by the world being a training ground for social unfoldment and inspired to see the healing as creative and evolutional.

Evolutional healing is built upon knowing there is somewhere to go, something to become. Healing is making whole. It brings about a move from a limited condition to a new level of a higher order of mental, emotional, physical, and spiritual wellbeing. Wounds are experienced as doorways to higher consciousness and more evolved forms.

As healers, social artists help us access our inner wisdom, moving us beyond the polarities of left versus right, us against them, and promoting cooperation, understanding, and networks of mutual aid. This challenge to the very canons of our human condition requires us all becoming evolutionary partners with each other.

In the intracultural and educational work we've done in many countries, we try to discover the main stories, myths, legends, and teaching tales that underlie the spirit of the culture in which we are working. Then we present them as the backdrop upon which to weave our work in human development. We find that people go further as well as faster and deeper if their learning is attached to a story and, most especially, if that story is a key myth of their culture.

In India we have worked with the Ramayana (a Sanskrit epic of ancient India) and the life of Gandhi; in Australia with certain Aboriginal creation myths; in England with stories of Percival, Gawain, and the other Knights of the Round Table's search for the Grail, in Bangladesh with the poetry of Tagore and other Bengali poets.

One feels instinctively when a new story is needed, when the old stories no longer speak to the current reality. What we need is for stories to be remythologized and rewoven in the light of today's necessities. This has always been the job of culture, to discover again and on a deeper level, the meaning and relevancy of the once and future story—for without story, a culture becomes denatured and demoralized.

Reweaving our stories in the light of today's necessities is exactly what this insightful and much needed book offers, in identifying all the motifs and archetypes for discovering the relevancy of the new story of our evolving consciousness.

We are at that stage where the real work of humanity begins. Partnering with Creation in the re-creation of ourselves, and in the restoration of the biosphere, we can bring into being a culture of kindness where we are all reconnected and fully engaged in our world. Think of yourself as a social artist, a conscious storyteller, following the creative force to bring others together, to do good in every situation that arises.

Prologue

A Pattern of Wholeness

Perhaps there is a pattern set up in the heavens
for one who desires to see it,
and having seen it, to find one in himself.
—Plato

A pattern perhaps found in the heavens and in us emerges as all things in the universe are seen as tied together, operating according to an overarching principle of wholeness.

Derived from a holistic worldview of balance and unity within the whole, this is expressed in the Hermetic principle of "That which is Below corresponds to that which is Above, and that which is Above corresponds to that which is Below, all things accomplishing the miracles of the One Thing."

This principle integrates all levels of reality from the macrocosm (the universe as a whole) to the microcosm (i.e., the human being, a miniature universe) and is upheld by the latest science and the earliest spiritual wisdom. It bridges the divide between duality and nonduality, confirms that the individual and the collective mirror one another in their essential nature and processes, and explains how all things are interconnected.

Imagine what it may have been like for the first Indigenous peoples seeking wisdom to live by. They seemingly observed a "pattern set up in the heavens" and wove this understanding of wholeness into the heart of the stories they told.

Now known as myths, their ancient stories established great truths and held communities together. Whether by metaphor, symbol, pattern, or repetition, their narratives offered a unifying framework for living within the flow of the natural world around them. These were unitive narratives, essential to their individual and collective well-being.

Across many millennia, however, communities expanded, spread out, became more diverse, and experienced conflict and disorder. Out of this discord emerged divisive narratives framed by a consciousness of duality that maintained separation and challenged the trajectory of the evolutionary impulse. Most of humanity's history has consisted of competing narratives fighting for the minds and hearts of people everywhere.

As we approach a consciousness of global integration, a new story of our wholeness is needed to frame this emerging interconnectedness. Humanity has arrived at a time when it is necessary for our own survival to come together again through unitive narratives. Such narratives would represent the unified nature of reality.

Because reality always has and will continue to exist as a unified field, and the earliest mystics and seers saw this and incorporated this understanding into their stories to live by, the story of wholeness is not new.

What is "new" is that the spiraling effect of the evolutionary impulse and our own evolving consciousness is becoming clearer by bringing us back to this innate, archetypal understanding. More of us now are becoming aware of this *as* a "new" story of wholeness. This book offers a new way of getting to and looking at the wholeness that always is. It does this by pulling together many threads of unitive narratives to identify their common pattern.

Stories that unify convey an inherent wholeness across all life forms, the natural world, and the entire creation. This understanding leads to the realization of a unitive consciousness, the goal of an evolving consciousness.

Unitive narratives invite us to embrace the wisdom of the complementarity, balance, and wholeness of seemingly opposing forces. This enables us to achieve unity in the diversity of forms and expressions we encounter on our way to a consciousness of wholeness. Binaries like feminine and masculine become more valued when they are viewed as human attributes rather than as a reason to divide us along gender lines.

Unitive narratives are needed now more than ever to lead us through a process of shifting the focus from individual wellbeing to collective wellbeing. In our time, the part no longer takes precedence over the whole. Both are completely interdependent. Exclusive emphasis upon any one part endangers the whole.

The purpose of this book is to provide the means for identifying and telling our own story of this wholeness as it emerges from a unitive consciousness. The creative process of exploring and expressing our own experience of wholeness gives us all a deeper commitment to ensuring Earth's well-being as a living organism, reveals to us the necessity of collaborative relationships and dynamic coevolutionary partnerships on a planetary scale, and confirms for us that our personal and collective evolution of consciousness depends on the stories we tell.

The pattern "set up in the heavens" and imbedded within us constantly assists our conscious evolution and confirms our wholeness on all levels. It encompasses a process of transformation that helps us move from beings endowed with an inherent potential to beings having fulfilled that potential.

A New Story of Wholeness was written to illustrate not only the universality of this pattern but also, more importantly, to guide us in becoming the whole beings we are meant to be, who recognize that this inner transformation serves a greater purpose in preparing us to be transformers of society.

This book provides a clearly focused set of guidelines that helps facilitate the process of personal and collective transformation already well under way. In *The Story of Our Time: From Duality to Interconnectedness to Oneness*, a 2017 Nautilus Book Award winner, I offered a narrative of the evolution of consciousness framed by seven unifying principles drawn from the world's wisdom traditions that traces love's unifying power guiding the collective transformation occurring now.

While *The Story of Our Time* shows how humanity is currently approaching the next step in its collective maturation by providing an overview of the larger, big picture narrative unfolding all around us, *A New Story of Wholeness* shows how the personal experience of this timeless pattern leads us directly into the process of collective transformation by guiding us toward contributing to the good of the whole.

What *The Story of Our Time* elucidates on the collective level, *A New Story of Wholeness* facilitates on the personal level by inviting you to identify, express, and share your own story of transformation as a vital part of the process of global transformation. Together, both illustrate how collective and individual transformation are so interdependent upon each other that they cannot be separated.

The introduction of *A New Story of Wholeness* provides an overview for identifying the qualities and characteristics of a new narrative of the evolutionary impulse. It unpacks the various formats of the core pattern of transformation designed for remembering and living into our innate wholeness. It inspires us to conceptualize our own journey from separation to union, from the many to the One, toward a recognition of our inherent wholeness.

Following this, a "Blueprint for Living Our Story of Wholeness"—a rich summary of the microcosm of a "pattern set up in the heavens"—serves as a reference tool throughout the entire process of telling your own version of this journey to wholeness.

The three main parts of this book are:

1) The meaning of the process, with three chapters looking at the primary principles of evolution, consciousness, and wholeness.

2) The pattern of the process, with three chapters explaining its parts: Call to Wholeness, Path of Purification, and Return to Wholeness.

3) The *Guide*, with a personal example to consider, keys for the process, and writing exercises providing all the needed roadmaps, tools, and understandings for identifying and telling your own story of living into wholeness. This practical, step-by-step process incorporates reflective writing exercises consisting of key points, prompts, a worksheet of personal experiences for all the archetypes and motifs, and instructions for compiling a narrative for each part of the pattern. The *Guide* provides everything needed for a do-it-yourself writing workshop. In addition, a "Meditation for Living into Wholeness" wraps up the *Guide* with a focused way to achieve the goal.

A New Story of Wholeness equips you to participate in the story of our time—a global movement of transformation leading to the unity in diversity of the entire human family—by identifying those experiences in your life that place you on a path to wholeness. Writing your own version of this new story of our evolving consciousness brings clarity and focus as you begin to recognize how your life's unfolding is part of something much larger.

With the Blueprint as our compass to point the way, we see not only the essence of the whole narrative pattern itself, but also how our own experiences follow this ancient, universal and, at the same time, *new* narrative we can all reclaim in this critical moment. Throughout the process, we are guided to become writers of our own unitive narrative engaging in the important work of conscious storytelling.

The key terms used throughout include *myth*, a metaphorical representation of a truth to live by; *story*, a weaving together of a sequence of events that may or may not be true; *narrative*, the form, structure, or pattern a myth or story is told in, usually connecting a system of personal or collective stories that may or may not be completed; and *unitive narrative*, a truthful personal or collective story of living into the wholeness of the unified field of existence all around us.

Wholeness is experienced in the qualities of completeness, harmony, balance, and unity within all the parts of a whole. Applying the principle of "as above, so below," all levels of whole systems co-exist as interdependent sub-systems within the Whole and are designed to maintain their own wholeness within that greater Whole as a complete wholeness-in-motion.

As a microcosm of the Whole, the human body is one such sub-system consisting of an organization of organs, all connected one to another, designed to function as a whole, each in harmony and balance with all the others, maintaining a fully functioning whole being. Cooperation is the principle that governs the functioning of the whole.

In the same way, as the health of the body is contingent upon the health and wholeness of every cell and every organ, so is the health of society contingent upon the unity and wholeness of the entire human family, both locally and globally.

Wholeness is the remedy for an ailing humanity. As Bahá'u'lláh stated, "Regard the world as the human body which, though at its creation whole and perfect, hath been afflicted, through various causes, with grave disorders and maladies… The mightiest instrument for the healing of all the world is the union of all its peoples."

We are the storytelling species. Let us reclaim our identity as whole beings living in harmony with all things around us and share widely our deeply lived stories of wholeness to bring us back together as a human family.

Introduction

A New Story of Our Evolving Consciousness

The evolution of existence is one.
The divine order is one.
All beings great and small
are subject to one law and one order.
—'Abdu'l-Bahá

Imagine all things in all of existence making up an interconnected whole, a oneness in which everything in the whole is an inseparable part. All things are of this wholeness-in-motion, nothing is ever separate from the whole.

In this divine order, everything is dependent upon what Teilhard de Chardin called a "single energy at play in the world." This holistic view of reality, with all things above corresponding to all things below, and "all things accomplishing the miracles of the One Thing," renders all seeming differences and distinctions imaginary.

Everything here is so interdependent that apparent opposites—like yin and yang, feminine and masculine—are complementary, interrelated halves of the same whole, balancing, integrating, uniting, and transcending their own duality.

Lao Tzu calls this wholeness of existence the "nameless," which is all there was at "the beginning of heaven and earth." In this original wholeness, as seen through a unitive consciousness, all things are sacred, revered, in harmony with all other things, without divisions, and in perfect relationship.

In this world of wholeness, such a unitive awareness serves to maintain and embed a consciousness of wholeness within us. It is central to Indigenous wisdom traditions, a state of consciousness sought by all contemplative practices, and a unifying field of awareness available to all.

Now imagine the story of Earth's origins. All existence was intended to remain forever whole. Adding intrigue to mystery, however, the evolution of existence took a detour in the Garden of Eden with the eating of the forbidden fruit. Or, in another version of this narrative, in Greek mythology, with the opening of Pandora's Box.

Re-imagine, if you will, this story as asserting our own individual will over a greater will not only bringing forth an archetype that introduced separation and opposition into the world, but also signaling humanity's fall from wholeness.

This separation of the "nameless" and the "named," the temporal and the eternal, fragmented the "named" into "ten thousand things," as Lao Tzu noted.

This fall from wholeness created two types of narratives, those that divide and those that unite. After millennia of stories focusing on duality and maintaining separation, what the world needs now is unitive narratives that will lead us through a process of returning to wholeness. This will be how all things are remembered as interconnected in one grand system of life in the cosmos.

This book identifies and highlights the key elements of many unitive narratives, brings them all into one storyline, and makes it evident that we are always integral components of that whole. It provides a way of remembering where we came from, who we are, and where we are going, while offering a step-by-step framework for reclaiming and living with a consciousness of wholeness.

Could a reunion of many unitive storylines be possible simply because there is only one timeless and universal narrative pattern shared by all of them? Could this be the same pattern Plato envisioned as set up in the heavens and within us as well?

Embedded within this pattern could be a genetic design to assist our evolution of consciousness. If so, it would bring about needed transformations to keep us on track, expand our consciousness toward a vision of the wholeness of all things, and keep our focus on this inherent wholeness all at the same time while also keeping humanity on its evolutionary trajectory.

Imagine, now, a world in which the explicit purpose of life is to realize the wholeness of the entire creation, to serve the good of the whole, to live our lives in wonderment of and in harmony with that whole.

The surah from the Quran (2:156), with variations in many sacred traditions, "We all come from God and unto Him do we return," often recited when a loved one dies, is much more than showing patience in God's supreme power.

On a mystical level, this saying encourages a nondual awareness within a duality-dominated world. Though we live in a realm of apparent separation, it assures us of a reunion while at the same time giving us a process of moving toward a consciousness of this underlying wholeness.

This mystic return to our Source of being suggests an outline, or structure, for living a life of purpose and meaning within a pattern framed by a process of *knowing, forgetting,* and *remembering.* According to several sacred traditions, we innately *know* we have come from wholeness, but we are born into a realm that eventually causes us to *forget* what we once knew, and we spend our lives in search of what will enable us to *remember* what we once knew.

Our consciousness has its source in unity. This is where our search is designed to lead us back to. Remembrance not only gets us in touch with our soul, the source of that *knowing,* but is also at the heart of all spiritual practice and is designed to remind us of our changeless nature.

Remembrance is a meditation creating gratitude, awakening us to a lasting reality. The conscious effort to maintain this focus expands our view of the world and our role in it. Remembrance brings us back to the awareness of what our eternal identity is and who we really are at our essence; knowing our true identity is the key to living in wholeness.

Our quest for wholeness encompasses a process of *remembering* our wholeness. This already exists, but we need a process designed to bring us back to this wholeness. The separation we experience here is based on a limited reading of reality. The illusion of separation comes into play because we tend to focus on temporal expressions of who we think we, or others, are, rather than on the lasting forms of existence.

Reality is the interconnected whole of all existence, with one common source and one guiding force, whose essence is unknowable. Instead of seeing this whole first, the human tendency is to create distinctions between things that are complementary parts of the whole.

When we become aware of this tendency, all perceived differences can become catalysts for our own spiritual growth, as life's difficulties, struggles, and challenges contribute most to meaning making, pattern shaping, and rediscovering who we are.

The return to our original state of oneness with the Creator occurs as we experience a pattern of archetypal (universally human) circumstances designed to expand and focus our consciousness on this inherent wholeness. This is the pattern that informs and supports our lifelong journey of returning to wholeness.

The oppositions and divisions all around us exist to stretch our consciousness until we see their deeper unity, their inherent wholeness. This understanding of the wholeness of all things spotlights the compassion, love, and grace that underlies all of creation and propels everything toward the fulfillment of a single purpose. St. Catherine of Genoa expresses how opposites become one:

> *O love, thy bonds are so sweet and so strong*
> *That they bind angels and saints together...*
> *In this union there is no difference between rich and poor,*
> *between nation and nation;*
> *all contradiction is excluded,*
> *for by this love crooked things are made straight*
> *and difficulties reconciled.*

Life is a mystic journey—a quest for the union of opposites—resulting in an abiding love within which we live every moment of our lives in wonderment of wholeness. The journey to uncover a hidden wholeness within us leads to this all-embracing unity of the whole.

We may feel alone in this quest for spiritual evolution, as this is the road not taken by most; but we are not the only ones. As many who understand unitive consciousness and its unfolding, evolving nature, this appears in just a few people at first and then more and more join in as consciousness continues to evolve. We may be pioneers now, but this path will eventually become well-trodden.

Rather than being solitary, the quest to live in wholeness is an intergenerational, international, interspiritual path, a superhighway meant for everyone. On this path, we discover our lives are directed toward experiences that naturally and purposely bring about personal and collective transformation.

When we start to live our lives consciously and deliberately, universal motifs and archetypes making up a timeless pattern can't help but to emerge, through which we discover not only *who* we are but also *why* we are deeply connected to all others.

What's also "new" about the story of wholeness that mystics and seers have been telling all along is that the process of living into wholeness—remembering who we really are at our essence—can now be seen not only as a pattern to follow but also as a code that has been broken wide open by myth, ritual, mysticism, psychology, and many other ways of knowing.

All of these embody a pattern with a process of transformation at its core designed to lead us out of a cave where illusions prevail and into the field where the light of wholeness is clearly visible.

In mythology, a version of this path was made popular by Joseph Campbell who pulled together the archetypes of the world's myths to form the pattern he called the monomyth, or the journey of the hero.

This pattern consists of a process of *departure – initiation – return* and is well known as leading to transformation through breaking away from the familiar, entering the unknown, encountering difficulties, undergoing a symbolic death, followed by a rebirth and renewal resulting in the restoration and rebalancing of the whole.

In ritual, Arnold van Gennep identified the pattern that all rites of passage follow as *separation – transition – incorporation*. This parallels very closely the process of myth while designed to guide the young person from a dependent state through independence and on to interdependence within one's community.

Christian scholar and writer Evelyn Underhill did for mysticism what Joseph Campbell would do for mythology fifty years later. She described "the mystic way" as a universal, androgynous journey of spiritual transformation following a pattern that leads from awakening to purification to illumination to a Dark Night of the Soul to union, a state of living in harmony with the whole.

In psychology, Carl Jung called this the "individuation process." It consists of the conscious experience of the archetypes we are born with, embedded in our psyche, or unconscious, bubbling up from within, released by life experiences, making us aware of their innate existence, and enabling the merging of opposites into a new whole.

Though the individuation process involves great struggle, as we will see in chapter 5, the experience of these archetypes helps direct our thoughts and actions in new ways that re-enforce our understanding of wholeness. In psychological terms, this is a process involving the *birth of the ego – death of the ego – birth of the whole self.*

All these variations on the same pattern, and more, emerge from the familiar narrative pattern of beginning – middle – end. Yet, on a deeper level this is a pattern that takes us through all manner of possible challenges in life for the sole purpose of preparing us to understand and accept the destined outcome resulting in a reclamation of our innate wholeness.

The pattern can therefore be most succinctly represented as *beginning – muddle – resolution*, where the muddle is the crisis, or challenge, really appearing as an opportunity, to prepare us for completing our personal journey to wholeness. This is precisely what makes possible the individual and collective evolutional healing Jean Houston referred to in the foreword.

Although Joseph Campbell presented the monomyth, or hero's journey, as both an inner and outer journey, it became better known as an external journey focusing on encountering and overcoming difficulties "out there."

Having met Joseph Campbell, who became my mentor, during a transformative time in my mid-twenties (which I will say more about in the *Guide*), I learned first-hand from him how my own experiences at the time fit this pattern—which also made more sense of them. I have since come to see this pattern as broader and deeper than personal transformation itself, even larger than any one container can hold.

Adding these mythological elements to mysticism, ritual, and psychology, the Blueprint for Living Our Story of Wholeness includes the "named" and the "nameless," the temporal and the eternal, as the itinerary taken leads us through both heaven and earth.

The pattern of the journey to wholeness provides a model that gets to the core of what we are made for. It contains all we need to fulfill our innate potential. Every single human being on the planet can realize the fruits of living this pattern and can become conscious of its meaning. In doing so, we benefit others as well by passing on its understanding and transforming the world in the process.

The universal pattern guiding our living into wholeness is a roadmap for achieving the greatest expansion of consciousness that is humanly possible. It is first and foremost an all-human inner journey that unites us all as conscious storytellers sharing our experience of returning to our innate wholeness.

As Joseph Campbell's *The Hero with a Thousand Faces* became more and more popular, a gender-based split developed between how men understood it and how women understood it. Many men took it literally as a "hero's" journey that became a great adventure story with overwhelming odds to beat and challenges to overcome out there in the world. Many women saw it as missing their experience of what their life is really about, and so distinct versions of a "heroine's" journey appeared.

In the process, there was a separation of potentialities and archetypes into masculine and feminine categories. This view keeps apart what we all have access to as human beings, having more in common with each other than we acknowledge.

We have much to learn from each other about how all the archetypes are human potentialities, not *either* feminine *or* masculine. Keeping them separate runs the risk of letting the whole get lost in its parts.

Living into the "new" story of our wholeness—the process of remembering who and what we are—removes the perceived boundaries between masculine and feminine, to show they are vestiges of our long history of living with a consciousness of duality.

This book, with the universal and timeless pattern it demystifies, is meant to re-unite the hero's journey and the heroine's journey into a single journey that returns us all to our inherent wholeness, with a unitive consciousness.

The process of remembering our wholeness fulfills who we are as human beings, and what we all share as members of one human family. It eliminates the choice of either/or, *either* masculine *or* feminine, and upholds the integrity of both/and, emphasizing all qualities and characteristics we have in common as human beings.

This also defines a process that is both writ small, for all individuals, and writ large, for civilization as a whole. As 'Abdu'l-Bahá, son and successor to Bahá'u'lláh, notes, all are subject to the same divine order.

We know we are well into the process of remembering our wholeness when the eternal breaks through from the temporal realm, when light merges with dark, and when polarities are consciously acknowledged and confronted in our everyday lives.

When these opposites are experienced, and their lessons learned in the classroom of the world, we remember what we came here for, and we evolve as we are intended to. We become the woodcarver who sees the tree spirits wanting to be fashioned even before the tree is carved, in what is already there yet invisible.

All the fleeting chaos, confusion, conflict, and suffering resulting from the interaction of opposites we experience here provide us with the jarring contrast between what will pass and what will last.

As we communicate more with the inner realm, we become fully aware of when the eternal bursts forth from the unconscious, giving us a timeless understanding that countless others have experienced before us.

Living into our wholeness results in a deeply lived life, having wrestled with our demons, danced with our angels, made plans with our inner guide, and connected with our soul. Only the fullest evolution of our own consciousness fulfills our greatest desire and potential.

In this process, we discover that, at our essence, we are more like others than not. This prepares us for the most satisfying thing we can experience—the sense of union with creation that comes through service to, and deep interpersonal relationships with, others.

The real goal of the process of remembering our unitive consciousness is not escape from the world, or even union with the Creator, but the fullest possible spiritual development through our work in the world.

The ongoing work of repairing the world, of restoring the world to wholeness, as in the Kabbalist tradition of Tikkun Olam is rooted in personal transformation. The part and the whole are so intricately connected that they cannot be separated. Personal transformation leads to world transformation, which prepares more individuals to be ready for personal transformation. Both are two aspects of the same ongoing process of uniting the whole. This is why 'Abdu'l-Bahá says service to humanity is prayer in action.

What differentiates the journey of living into wholeness from other unitive narratives it derives from is that its deeper purpose leads not only to individual wholeness but also to collective wholeness, as its outcome carries the function of acting in the world in a way that leads to collective transformation and the betterment of the whole, all in one process.

The pattern we often instinctively live out from within not only makes everything possible for us, but it also means that a great deal depends upon us. In fact, carrying out our individual responsibility to the whole is what ensures the periodic renewal of the whole.

Our awareness of this responsibility brings with it the burden of its fulfillment. Giving back to others something of what we have been given "does not shut one out from the world, but gathers the world to oneself," as Jung said.

This understanding tells us that our own experience is greater than ourselves. We may even feel, as Jung also said, that "we are no longer individuals but the race," and, with the utmost humility, that "the voice of all mankind resounds in us."

This voice of the whole is emerging as a new story of our unity and connectedness. A half century ago, Joseph Campbell provided some guidelines for such a new narrative when he said that a living, "creative" mythology, relevant to this "fresh" new world, would serve the four functions of bringing us more into accord with ourselves, others, the mystery of life, and the universe around us.

He called these functions the *psychological* (which guides us through an integrated life); the *social* (which validates and maintains evolving moral norms); the *cosmological* (which offers an image of the universe in accord with the knowledge of the time); and the *mystical* (which awakens and maintains in us a sense of awe, humility, respect, and gratitude in recognition of that ultimate mystery).

Together, these four functions serve a unitive function. They are the necessary qualities, components, and characteristics of a unitive narrative needed to guide our individual and collective process of living into wholeness, the parameters for evaluating a unitive narrative that would direct us toward the next level of our evolving consciousness.

A unitive narrative for our time, meant to guide and inspire us all, will be alive, in harmony with the evolutionary flow, upholding the latest scientific discoveries and spiritual revelations, bridging interpersonal and social divides, contributing to unity in diversity, and integrating all things in the entire cosmos. A unitive narrative will return us to wholeness, providing hope all the way.

The threads of this new story we experience in our own lives are the common threads that we share with all of humanity. Yet, the process described in following this universal pattern is more metaphor than literal. What keeps us on the track of living into our own story of wholeness is an innate blueprint we are all born with (see the Blueprint for Living Our Story of Wholeness following this introduction).

Each of us lives this pattern out in our own unique way. Our version may be woven slightly differently than others, with a personal twist here or there. The part is always a reflection of the whole, the two together telling one narrative of the transformation to wholeness.

In our own version of a unitive narrative, we find the symbols of our common humanity. Its meaning is metaphorical and multi-layered. Within it is also found our most deeply held truth. A unitive narrative speaks to us through qualities that are transformative; its meaning is in the process that has led us to a consciousness of wholeness.

All the possibilities of the evolution of consciousness pre-exist in our collective unconscious as archetypes. They are emerging into our consciousness more rapidly now in this time of great change and transformation. Living into this timeless blueprint, the spiritual DNA we all share, is the surest way to achieve our fullest potential—which will also bring us all closer to our common destiny.

This is how we become conscious storytellers, by knowing we are both the story and the teller of a uniquely powerful narrative imbedded within us to build unity across differences and forge wholeness where separation appears. The mindful storyteller creates a space for love and harmony to spread across the planet.

Our own new story of living into wholeness tells in numerous ways how the collective guides the personal and the personal serves the collective, a process in which the primary motifs and archetypes of cooperation, harmony, and unity become the building-blocks of a new world.

At the deepest level of understanding lies a unitive consciousness. As the storytelling species, it is our deepest desire to express a unitive narrative that tells of our own experience of wholeness. Remember, you are the *story* and the *teller*. It is my hope that by following these threads you will discover a path leading to living into your fullness.

Blueprint for Living Our Story of Wholeness

Key Motifs and Archetypes

Call to Wholeness

Waking up to something beyond what we've known, we embark on a journey to a higher consciousness, as our destiny unfolds toward our innate potential.

In unknown realms, we find we are being guided, protected, and assisted on our way.

As new challenges appear, impending difficulties recede and fade as we proceed.

Following a need to withdraw, retreat, turn inward, or cut ourselves off from the world, a desire to develop and evolve in the world grows within us.

Path of Purification

As our consciousness expands, we open up to greater challenges as they come our way, to the glimpses of the new reality we are witnessing, and to fulfilling our inner potential.

Recognizing more instances of guidance and assistance coming our way, we discover more of our innate capacity, and are intent on cleaning up, integrating, unifying, and healing all parts of ourselves to reclaim our innate wholeness.

Though living in the realm of dualities, our consciousness of wholeness grows stronger. Challenges, tests, and temptations serve to solidify our values and standards.

Fear of letting go of the old way of seeing things dissolves; we die to the limited self, and are renewed and reborn, more than we were, with a full consciousness of oneness.

With our fullest potential in reach, we also understand that we are still quite vulnerable.

Return to Wholeness

Focused on sustaining the unitive consciousness we are convinced of as the highest reality, we embrace showing up for all this demands of us, including giving back to others what we have been given, lifting up others along their journey, and linking up with others to serve the evolutionary impulse and the good of the whole.

Our return to wholeness is facilitated by knowing consciously the struggle of having transcended temporal boundaries and finding our own balance.

We remember that we are always in the process of becoming, interdependent and interconnected with all others.

We seek to maintain a holistic view of reality, as we take on a wider, all-inclusive identity, and integrate more all-human qualities, characteristics, and virtues into our thoughts and actions.

We strive to live as the whole being we are, lighting up the path we walk, and looking upon all things with the eye of wholeness.

Part One
Meaning — Healing the Illusion of Separation

Our present world is conditioned
by our present mode of consciousness;
only when that consciousness passes from its
present dualistic mode
conditioned by time and space
will the new creation appear,
which is the eternal reality of which our world is a mirror.

—Bede Griffiths

1 The Evolution Principle

As man advances in civilization...
he ought to extend his social instincts and sympathies
to the people of all nations and races.
—Charles Darwin

O ur understanding of evolution, of how things develop according to their inner nature, and whether there is an underlying direction and order to this, has unfolded gradually. This is because we understand the world we live in, its movement and direction, by the consciousness we bring to it.

Our consciousness is extremely challenged in these times of misinformation, fake news, and deep divides. But there have been times like this before. Evolution's path has never been a straight line. It unfolds with built-in ups and downs, spiraling toward renewal. We're seeing this with ongoing refugee crises, racial inequality, political strife, and military clashes across the globe. Though these are apparent side-steps, or even back-sliding, evolution's direction always, eventually, moves toward the good of the whole.

As Ken Wilber's Integral Theory notes, there is a direction to culture in which stages of growth unfold purposefully. He says, "like all other living systems, we humans are in the process of *growing toward our own highest potential*." If we see evolution as "Spirit-in-action," this is "destined to carry all of us straight to the Divine."

A holistic look at the entirety of cultural evolution, including what is yet to come, reveals this to be a process consisting of three essential steps: moving from unity to plurality, and, at some point, back to unity, or *wholeness* followed by *duality* followed by *wholeness*.

Consider these three phases of cultural evolution. First, the earliest Indigenous communities were inherently unified by virtue of their common traditions, beliefs, and need to maintain their way of life. They integrated conflict into their community life with an overarching consciousness of their *oneness* as well as the wholeness of all things around them.

Then, as communities expanded, spread out, and global migration became the norm, societies became more complex. This caused cultures to experience conflict and deeper discord with each other that was more challenging to resolve. Competing knowledge systems created the illusion of separation, transforming human thinking into a pervasive consciousness of *duality* to reflect the introduction of greater chaos and struggle in daily life.

This shift in consciousness led to a painful process over many millennia of diverse communities dealing with differences in ways that escalated into systemic practices of segregation, prejudice, oppression, racism, conquest, genocide, and ultimately war.

Duality became the lens through which humans have viewed everything since the great migration. This extended period of differentiation, however, saw circles of unity continue to expand, from unity in the family, to the clan, to the city, and to the nation. But across each of these circles, an "us" and a "them" continued to create differences.

Finally, out of necessity for our collective survival, humanity is now faced with an unprecedented challenge: to establish unity on the global level. This phase of our cultural evolution will require us to reclaim our intended consciousness of *oneness*, characterized by a focus on the collective "we," not a "me" or even a "them."

We are closer now to reclaiming our unity on the largest scale than ever before. This is where our process of evolution has been leading us. Living with the realization of our interdependency as one human community with one common heritage and destiny is the only sustainable worldview left for us to embrace.

Humanity's greatest current need—and opportunity—is to transcend a prevailing, unsustainable consciousness that divides, creates hierarchies, and endangers our very survival. We face a crisis of consciousness that threatens the evolutionary impulse and distorts the way we relate to each other and the natural environment.

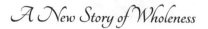

> ## The Evolution Principle
>
> ***Evolution is directional, toward ever wider circles of unity.***
> *In all realms, all things are tied together,*
> *and evolve through a process of*
> *maturation, decline, and eventual renewal,*
> *always toward their inherent potential.*
>
> From *The Story of Our Time* by Robert Atkinson

A large part of this present crisis goes back a century and three-quarters to the misunderstanding of Charles Darwin's theory of evolution. Social Darwinists turned evolution upside down, focusing only on the survival of the fittest and the competition needed to sustain that. This fueled generations of oppression, which led to segregation, racism, genocide, and most wars.

Darwin had much to say about social evolution, as well as biological evolution. In 1859, his groundbreaking *The Origin of Species* brought biological evolution into popular discourse. As a former divinity school student, he also embraced the idea that all life comes from the same source and is part of the great Tree of Life.

His pioneering work opened the door to an awareness that all things evolve, even on the social and cultural level. As evolutionary biologist David Sloan Wilson has said, Darwin needs to be most remembered for his view that it is cooperation, not competition, that leads to larger and larger circles of unity.

In 1871, in *The Descent of Man*, Darwin clearly stated his view of social evolution built upon cooperation at each level:

> As man advances in civilization, and small tribes are united into larger communities, the simplest reason would tell each individual that he ought to extend his social instincts and sympathies to all members of the same nation, though personally unknown to him. This point being reached, there is only an artificial barrier to prevent his sympathies extending to the men of all nations and races.

This shows that social evolution is directed toward a familiar and long-desired outcome, extending the natural law of cooperation and the Golden Rule from the individual level to the global level. Yet, Darwin's grand vision of social evolution would require a leap of individual consciousness leading to a leap in collective consciousness.

Interestingly, just prior to this, in the mid-1800s, the Bahá'í writings reconciled the two prevailing views of evolution and divine creation by first providing a perspective that merged both into a view of evolution explaining how all life evolves gradually. 'Abdu'l-Bahá explained the nature of evolution this way:

> ... the growth and development of all beings proceeds by gradual degrees. This is the universal and divinely ordained law and the natural order. The seed does not suddenly become the tree; the embryo does not at once

become the man… all these grow and develop gradually until they attain the limit of perfection… The law of God is one; the evolution of existence is one; the divine order is one. All beings great and small are subject to one law and one order.

Then, 'Abdu'l-Bahá explained further that because all things are interconnected, having originated from the same Source, cooperation and reciprocity are the true catalysts for evolution:

… all beings are linked together like a chain; and mutual aid, assistance, and interaction are among their intrinsic properties, the cause of their formation, development and growth. Through numerous proofs and arguments every single thing has an effect and influence upon every other, either independently or through a causal chain.

Finally, because of this common origin, all processes of evolution are governed by the same natural law, with all things following a similar trajectory:

… nature is subject to a sound organization, to inviolable laws, to a perfect order, and to a consummate design … all are subject to one universal law from which they never depart.

Evolution is thus determined by universal law, a design which all things follow. This principle of evolution is confirmed by the world's wisdom traditions, as expressed in the words of the Buddha, "*All things originate from one essence, develop according to one law, and are destined to one aim.*"

A 2016 article in Science Magazine entitled "What is the Most Astounding Fact about the Universe?" further confirmed this view of evolution, stating that the most astounding fact about the universe is that the entire universe obeys the same fundamental laws of nature.

When the latest views of both science and religion are taken into account, we see there is a direction to evolution, leading toward larger and larger circles of unity. The purpose of evolution is to build cooperation and unity across ever-expanding circles. Evolution directs us toward the union of the whole.

With reality as one, and harmony as a guiding principle, the Laws of Nature express observable and constant patterns which tie all things together in an indivisible oneness. Surrounding and embracing everything is an interconnected whole.

A holistic view sees the whole first, and evolution as part of a single great process encompassing the entire creation. Yet, as evolution in all realms is a gradual process of growth, we often miss the variations, or the ups and the downs, in the process. A big picture view of evolution not only notices these, but also acknowledges that evolution does not happen in a straight, smooth, linear fashion.

Evolution includes—and is sustained by—seemingly opposing forces interacting with each other to facilitate a process of transformation that is needed to expand circles of harmony. This dialectical, oppositional process is a catalyst to transformation. Adversity is built into the process of evolution, not as an impediment but as a crucial element leading to the transcendence of duality. Unity is the outcome of this natural process of restoring those seemingly opposing forces to their wholeness.

Evolution on all levels, personal and social, is carried out through unfolding stages between which transformation propels further progress. Evolution is not *either* linear progress *or* linear regress (as may appear to be the case when the clash between apparent opposing forces is at its greatest). A holistic view integrates it all into a spiral-like unfolding that is always evolving toward higher and higher levels.

Leading systems thinker Ervin Laszlo explains this by referring to the view of Bahá'u'lláh, the nineteenth century Persian prophet and founder of the Bahá'í Faith, who proclaimed that "the oneness of mankind will be achieved in evolutionary stages replete with strife, chaos, and confusion." Laszlo says this emerging concept of historical progress is "less naïve and more realistic than the linear progress or regress concept dominant in public consciousness."

"The next stage in social evolution," Laszlo continues, still referring to Bahá'u'lláh's teachings, "is the organization of human society as a planetary civilization which will be characterized by the emergence of a world community, the consciousness of world citizenship, and the founding of a global culture allowing for an infinite diversity in the characteristics of its components."

But this consummation of human evolution will come about through periods of upheaval. As Bahá'u'lláh wrote toward the end of the 19th century, "winds of despair" are blowing in every direction. The strife that divides and afflicts humanity is increasing, as are the signs of impending convulsions.

This divinely inspired non-linear perspective that Laszlo refers to is aligned with the scientific view that emerged in the late 20th century from other leading systems thinkers, as well. If we recognize this non-linear evolutionary trend for what it is, understand where it is ultimately leading us, and commit to live and *act* in accordance with this evolutionary impulse, we will become the co-creators of what we seek.

Meaningful evolution is only possible with this confrontation and union of opposites. Science and religion recognize a common force guiding evolutionary progress toward a consciousness of wholeness. Both emphasize the interconnected nature of all things as part of the same reality.

This is the new story of humanity's evolving consciousness. A goal of all sacred traditions, and now of most of science as well, is moving beyond the illusion of dualities that dominate the temporal world and toward the wholeness that always is.

With humanity's collective evolution built upon a spiraling process directing the expansion of consciousness, we can better understand that periods of conflict are built into evolution. Times of struggle, like these we are in now, slow down and sometimes temporarily impede progress. Yet, they are nevertheless followed by a growth spurt.

What accounts for those periodic growth spurts, as the Parliament of the World's Religions said in their 1993 document, *Towards a Global Ethic*, is a transformation of consciousness: "Earth cannot be changed for the better unless the *consciousness* of individuals is changed." This has always been the pattern, built upon a process of transformation, that facilitates evolution on both the collective and individual levels. And this is where the consciousness principle takes over.

2 *The Consciousness Principle*

The germ of the transcendent life,
the spring of the amazing energy which enables the great
mystic to arise to freedom,
is latent in all of us, an integral part of our humanity.
—Evelyn Underhill

Consciousness is the dynamic unfolding of a systematic awareness of ourselves in relation to others and the world, and how we make sense of it all. There is a rich and deep well of nourishment waiting to guide us through this journey.

The good news is that the transformation of consciousness—seen by the Parliament of the World's Religions as what is most needed now—is an inherent potential always within us all.

The consciousness we strive for is innate, embedded in our unconscious mind, as archetypes, waiting to be called forth, to light our way, to guide us toward the truth we seek, and provide us with a direction for the life we want to live.

Achieving our innate potential is the greatest challenge we face as humans. Our biological, intellectual, moral, and spiritual development is designed to unfold in degrees and stages, transcending each seeming limit we face, bringing this potential into being gradually.

Though subject to the same natural law as all of Creation, the fulfillment of consciousness does not come easily; it is not guaranteed. A conscious effort is required to expand our consciousness, even as greater and greater levels of comprehension of self, society, the mysteries of life, and the wonders of the universe are explored.

A consciousness of wholeness, which is the natural outcome of our own potential and perfection, depends upon the initiative we take to actively investigate reality on our own. Inherent in this process are myriad distractions that capture our attention and pull us in other directions, away from where our evolving consciousness would naturally take us.

But the forces of the universe are always operating to liberate our consciousness from previously restricted stages and propel it onward in its evolution. Nothing expands our consciousness more than the proactive conscious search for truth. Now more than ever, it is the independent investigation of reality that will unleash our fullest potential, leading to the spiritualization of human consciousness. The awakening of new capacities is bringing with it the recognition of new responsibilities for a collective maturity that are restructuring society.

We are born into a mystery that sometimes captures our attention, and sometimes not. Sometimes, when we least expect it, that mysterious realm all around us seems to sneak up on us and pull at our heartstrings.

As Elizabeth Gilbert wrote in *Eat, Pray, Love*, hidden somewhere within us is "the itch, the mad and relentless urge to want to understand the workings of existence." When acknowledged, this can become a single-minded quest nothing can deter us from. Its destination is inner peace, serenity, and a quiet mind.

This is a universal potential, yet its opposite, what the Vedanta and Buddhist teachings call *maya*, our tendency to be swayed toward what turns out to be an illusion or a deception, still prevents most of humanity from recognizing reality in its true form.

The Consciousness Principle

Consciousness is an innate potentiality
unfolding toward right relationships on all levels.
Yet, consciousness is dependent upon
the initiative we take to actively investigate reality.

From *The Story of Our Time* by Robert Atkinson

Because we get distracted, we must search for this reality, Gilbert says, as we would for water if our head were on fire. To seek truth is to be open to what is beyond us, to connecting and aligning with what is greater than us.

There are built-in cognitive structures that guide our way on this journey, what Jung calls archetypes, or types of inherited behavior, that provide us with our innate potential, giving us more strength and courage every step of the way. What these archetypes really carry for us is quite remarkable, as Jung explains, "The collective unconscious contains the whole spiritual heritage of humanity's evolution, born anew in the brain structure of every individual."

One of the first of these archetypes that human beings ever experienced is the Call, a theme as old as story itself. It is ubiquitous to all literature and the most common basis for all narrative plots. Classic mythology and fairy tales are framed by the motif of search. All the world's mythic heroes and heroines were the original seekers after truth, leading them down a path they were designed to follow.

The archetype of the Call, as we'll see in chapter 4, consists of a quest that separates us from the familiar and signals that our destiny is unfolding. Its purpose is to expand our consciousness, the necessary first step on the path that leads to the realization of our potential, through transformation and renewal.

The call to an awakened consciousness is one of the most important needs of our time. Only by this conscious effort to follow the Call can the potential of consciousness be realized. As consciousness evolves, it changes the way we see everything, helping us to fulfill our purpose of grasping the sacred nature of reality.

As we strive toward the perfections within us to reach the spiritual capacity we are endowed with and integrate these experiences into our own life, a new chapter to the ongoing story of our evolving consciousness will be written.

The search for truth leads us toward interconnectedness and wholeness. We are guided by the most powerful force in the universe—love—to seek integration, communion, and wholeness. In fulfilling this potentiality, the power of our own consciousness, reflecting upon itself, reveals how connected we all are.

This provides us with a seamless, unified worldview consisting of one reality; it is how we come to know that our life is part of every other life, and therefore in harmony with Creation. The search for truth changes the way we see everything and gives us a more expansive window into the sacred nature of existence. If we are satisfied with what has been handed down to us, we will remain complacent and inert. But if we continually seek the unknown and make it known, new knowledge will guide our way to the perennial truth of oneness.

This search for truth is a key principle of a timeless wisdom that recognizes the individual soul as a reflection of divine reality. Once the life of the spirit, or the quest of the soul, begins, it is never without progress. Spiritual discernment, development, and search always bring us closer to the Creator.

The world's sacred traditions assure us of this: "Seek and ye shall find..." (Christian tradition). "If thou shalt seek the Lord, thou shalt find him..." (Jewish tradition). "The nature of the one Reality must be known by one's own clear spiritual perception; it cannot be known through a pundit..." (Shankara, Hindu Vedanta).

In the Islamic tradition we have: "He who approaches near to Me one span, I will approach near to him one cubit..." and from the Baháʼí tradition: "If we investigate the religions to discover the principles underlying their foundations, we will find they agree, for the fundamental reality of them is one and not multiple."

In our time, the search for truth, the investigation of reality, has been made a primary spiritual principle, and the most important of all human rights. Exercising this right can bring us the greatest of benefits. It not only expands and fulfills our individual consciousness, it also is the means for advancing civilization.

What all these sacred traditions have in common about unleashing this latent potential is that this process results in a balance of energies between seemingly opposing forces— masculine/feminine, Shiva/Shakti, Yang/Yin, or Doing/Being— as we encounter both all along the way in our journey to wholeness.

This may be the only thing that will heal the perceived separation around us, as in our search for truth, in our quest to expand our consciousness, we come to a remarkable realization: we find that the goal of our search is the boundless consciousness that unites us with all beings, all of creation, and with divinity itself.

This is where a consciousness of wholeness leads us, and everyone expresses this in their own way, as did William Blake ("to see the universe in a grain of sand, and eternity in a moment"), Walt Whitman ("I am large, I contain multitudes"), and Tara Brach ("On this sacred path... we discover how to love ourselves into wholeness"). These are some of the countless expressions of knowing that the whole is *in* the part, the part is *of* the whole, and both are one.

All sacred traditions have their own practices and tools that are specifically designed to help us all get to this realization, whether it is prayer, meditation, deepening in the sacred writings, remembrance of God, yoga, ritual, initiation, whirling dance, vision quest, upholding the highest ethical standards, pilgrimage, seeing with the eye of oneness, service to others, and so many more.

A fullness of consciousness is far from guaranteed. Without conscious effort, we would remain blinded by the deceptions around us. There are those who hold on to a self-centered consciousness built on the illusion of separation and there are those who desire to live by a mature consciousness supporting the evolutionary impulse toward wholeness and unity.

This dichotomy results in a battle of consciousnesses. Humanity can be said to be in the midst of an all-out crisis of consciousness. A holistic view of our evolving consciousness sees such divisions arising from placing parts above the whole. Yet, they are differences of gradation rather than irreconcilable differences.

We are all capable of living into a consciousness of wholeness. A holistic perspective gives us the clear and vivid image of consciousness as a continuum along which we evolve as our experiences give us a broader and deeper perspective on the reality we live within.

The Consciousness Continuum

We all start out with an innate potential
but we can move in either direction
across the continuum

	Peace	Unity	Cooperation	Equality	Appreciation	Respect
Unity and Wholeness as the Guiding Principles:		global justice	unity in diversity	harmony	compassion	integrity
	collective security		gender equality	love	affinity	aspiration
A consciousness based on the oneness of all existence, supported by universal, unifying spiritual principles for the good of the whole.		economic equity		non violence	reverance for all life	
		universal human rights	racial harmony	the value of multiculturalism		
	world unity	conciousness of world citizenship	interfaith collaboration	inclusivity		
	global harmony	a wider, more inclsuive loyalty	philanthropy	altruism		
	... the oneness of humanity		ecological stewardship	universal education		

This holistic vantage point allows us to view all variations of consciousness as existing within the same whole at the same time. On this *consciousness continuum*, all states of consciousness are interconnected and interdependent, as links of a chain.

The consciousness continuum has two sides. One side is guided by a *consciousness of duality* which creates hierarchies, builds systems of injustice, and leads to stereotyping, discrimination, and violence, ending up with genocide and war, endangering our very survival as a species. This side of the continuum gives us a partial view of reality built upon separation.

The other side of the continuum is guided by a *consciousness of wholeness* which moves us from respect for difference toward

How Our Understanding of Reality
Leads Us in Opposite Directions

The attitudes, values, and principles
we live by determine whether
we end up with war or peace.

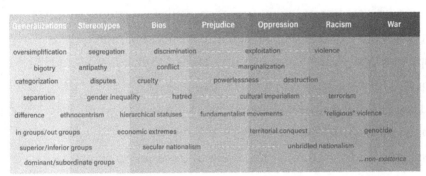

Generalizations	Stereotypes	Bias	Prejudice	Oppression	Racism	War
oversimplification	segregation	discrimination		exploitation	violence	**Separation and Duality as the Guiding Principles:**
bigotry	antipathy	conflict		marginalization		
categorization	disputes	cruelty	powerlessness	destruction		*A consciousness based on division, distinction, and discord, supported by dogmatic and exclusive principles for raising up the part.*
separation	gender inequality	hatred		cultural imperialism	terrorism	
difference	ethnocentrism	hierarchical statuses	fundamentalist movements		"religious" violence	
in groups/out groups		economic extremes		territorial conquest	genocide	
superior/inferior groups		secular nationalism			unbridled nationalism	
dominant/subordinate groups					...non-existence	

The Story of Our Time: From Duality to Interconnectedness to Oneness, by Robert Atkinson

compassion for all. Upholding universal human rights, gender equality, economic equity, and social justice leads to unity in diversity—all interconnected stepping-stones to peace. This side of the continuum gives us a holistic view of reality built upon wholeness and unity.

From the perspective of consciousness as a continuum, all things are seen as they are, aspects of one reality where all things in the entirety of Creation fit together as a unified field, a mysterious harmony, a hidden wholeness.

As our consciousness shifts to seeing the whole first, reality does not change, we do. As we change, we see the same reality differently. Viewing consciousness as a continuum gives a clear evolutionary path to the direction of life, toward a unitive view of all things connected.

The individual evolution of consciousness fuels the collective evolution of consciousness, moving the collective along the consciousness continuum toward peace. World unity is the only way to world peace. Unity is a prerequisite to peace; cooperation is a prerequisite to unity; equality is a prerequisite to cooperation; appreciation is a prerequisite to equality; respect is a prerequisite to appreciation. Peace through unity, cooperation, equality, and respect is the way we evolve toward lasting peace.

Having known duality, having even a glimpse of wholeness inspires us to turn our consciousness away from a segregated perspective and toward a unified view, to traverse the principle-centered, morally focused side of the continuum to realize the fullness of our interconnectedness as one species in harmony with all life.

This journey to wholeness may be the greatest antidote to prevent the current flood of false narratives from turning this into a "post-truth" world. Not to undertake this journey threatens our collective evolution of consciousness.

All the world's religious and spiritual traditions stress the importance of cultivating the capacity of consciousness through a practice that aligns us with the universal order. Meditation, reflection, and contemplative practice are some of the tools that enable us to access the deepest meaning of things.

Consciousness is a complex capacity comprising the powers of imagination (conceiving things), thought (reflecting upon realities), comprehension (understanding realities), and memory (remembering what we imagine, think, and understand), all of which 'Abdu'l-Bahá refers to as our spiritual powers.

Consciousness is our inner power, while sight, hearing, smell, taste, and touch are our five outer powers, the agents of perception. The mind is the intermediary between the outer and inner powers, connecting them both.

We strive, as best as we are able with the circumstances we are given, to realize the perfections embedded within us, to reach the spiritual capacity we are endowed with, and to develop the virtues of the soul—such as justice, equity, and goodness—so we can reach the heights of consciousness. Or, we remain within the opposing constrained expressions of the material self, falling short of our potential.

Carl Jung explained this process in his autobiography: "My life is a story of the self-realization of the unconscious. Everything in the unconscious seeks outward manifestation, and the personality too desires to evolve out of its unconscious conditions and to experience itself as a whole." This is why a new chapter in the ongoing story of our evolving consciousness is so needed. Our time calls for a renewal of the perennial truths that got us this far. Consciousness is a gift designed to help us see beyond what is evident, delve into the hidden meanings of the obvious, and extract the essence of what we are pondering.

We develop a second sight—the power of insight, intuition, and illumination by using the gift of consciousness to its fullest. Life is a process of moving from an underdeveloped, localized fragmented consciousness toward a fully developed universal, boundless, unitive consciousness.

To keep our consciousness always unfolding toward its innate potential, our fullest conscious attention is always needed, as the way we understand and relate to the reality around us is determined by the consciousness we bring to it. The consciousness we live with is our window into reality.

Jung points out an unexpected reward from this effort. "To find out what is truly individual in ourselves, profound reflection is needed; and suddenly we realize how uncommonly difficult the discovery of individuality in fact is." The power of our own consciousness, reflecting upon itself, reveals how connected we all are. This is exactly what Evelyn Underhill means when she says the germ of the transcendent life is latent in all of us.

Consciousness is a light spreading its love throughout the world, a magnet attracting all to its oneness, merging all into an all-embracing unity of the All. The only thing that changes in the journey from separation to wholeness is consciousness.

3 The Wholeness Principle

We are living cells in the living body of Earth.
Our collective body is in trauma and we are experiencing
that...
We need to listen to ourselves as if we are listening to a
message from the universe.
—Johanna Macy

All things are part of the same web of wholeness, yet we live as if all things are separate, and even at odds with each other. This illusion of separateness causes just about every problem, conflict, and even war, that humanity has ever known. It is also what has sustained a dominant divided consciousness.

Within this web of wholeness, all living things in the universe find realization through just one power that sustains all things. As Teilhard de Chardin noted, a single energy is at play in the world.

Reality—the entire Creation—and everything in it is always a whole. This holistic, nondual principle is at the heart of the world's mystic traditions. Because of this unified organization, consciousness evolves by the pull of this single energy toward this inherent wholeness. This is also why we innately respond to guiding principles that help us grasp the wholeness of the reality we live in.

The challenge we have is seeing the whole through its parts, bringing the whole back together, and living in the understanding of this wholeness. Uniting a divided consciousness into a consciousness of wholeness largely depends upon *experiencing* the wholeness that is always all around us.

As Deepak Chopra notes in the Afterword of this book, "wholeness lies beyond any kind of split or fragmentation. Wholeness is everything. It is the One, the All, or Brahman, as it was known in Vedic India. Wholeness offers only the experience of yourself as whole: as pure existence and pure consciousness."

This understanding brings us into the reality of wholeness. Consciousness, he says, ties everything in the entire universe together; it gives light its brightness and color, creates images in our mind's eye, and adds meaning to everything. Our overarching challenge in healing this false separation, which is the cause of all suffering, is making a complete shift in how we relate to reality.

If we can see the outer world as a distraction, an illusion, as ancient spiritual traditions did, we can focus on the one reality, which is a complete wholeness already, with everything existing within it.

It is the innate nature of consciousness to evolve toward its own inherent potential. When the acquired illusion of separation is replaced with innate wholeness, we open up to the experience of ourselves and the entire Creation as whole. Our paradox to resolve is that we live in a world dominated by dualities existing within a Creation characterized by nonduality. The many within the One.

The Wholeness Principle

Reality is one, and all of Creation is a whole.
Consciousness evolves toward this wholeness.

From *The Story of Our Time* by Robert Atkinson

Central to resolving this paradox is that for most of us, including mystics and mythic heroes and heroines, the journey from separation to wholeness takes us through a Dark Night of the Soul, a period of intense struggle and purification that precedes a deep transformative experience, as first noted by St. John of the Cross. This archetype is at the heart of the journey of living into wholeness.

In this historic moment, we're seeing one transformative archetype after another. The COVID-19 pandemic shut nearly everything down around us, pulling us into the mythical belly of the whale, where many of us withdrew into the unknown, giving us unexpected time for a retreat we didn't ask for.

This forced us to leave behind the familiar, turn inward, use the opportunity to reassess and reevaluate everything we thought we knew, and search for truth, taking us further into a transformational undertaking. All of this has shown us we are more connected than we thought.

Then, not yet out of our retreat, we found ourselves in the midst of a collective Dark Night of the Soul, as pandemic conditions spotlighted great injustices that needed to be confronted. We've not yet seen the light of dawn, but we know it is coming, as all the world's wisdom traditions foretell a time of harmony and peace on earth.

We are living in this moment for a reason. This universal, timeless archetypal pattern tells us a great transition is unfolding in the way we relate to each other in the world we share. As the Bahá'í writings affirm:

> *The current world confusion and calamitous condition in human affairs [is] a natural phase in an organic process leading ultimately and irresistibly to the unification of the human race in a single social order whose boundaries are those of the planet. The human race, as a distinct, organic unit, has passed through evolutionary stages analogous to the stages of infancy and childhood in the lives of its individual members, and is now in the culminating period of its turbulent adolescence approaching its long-awaited coming of age.*

This is the moment the visionaries and mystics of past ages have longed for. We are all here now to help build the future we envision. We're in a collective period of transformation, a collective near-death experience, a collective rebirth, that is guiding humanity as a whole to the highest level of consciousness ever known.

The voice of our collective soul calls out to us to wake up to the story of who we really are. We see this story unfolding now, being told every day through every act of kindness and compassion. This new story is showing us where we came from and what our common destiny is. Even while we experience fear, anxiety, tension, and conflict all around us now, this is preparing us for something greater. Emerging through the evolutionary impulse is a bright future.

The very nature of the evolution of consciousness—and the completion of the universal pattern embedded within transformation and renewal—gives us an abiding sense of hope, a living active hope that engages us with the process we are participating in, to assist it along, toward its fulfillment.

Humanity is coming of age. We're going through the turmoil of transition, from a difficult in-between period to our collective maturity, a time when we will live with a common purpose, in a just, prosperous, and peaceful world.

Helping to guide this process, we're experiencing the conscious confrontation of opposing forces, a ubiquitous dialectic creating a dynamic tension that is with us every day of our lives. It shapes the most fundamental processes of human and social development, balancing stability and change.

This is the heart of a process of transformation, a basic struggle within each stage of personal and collective development that creates an essential opposition designed to generate and facilitate growth. Life is made up of an on-going series of conflicts and struggles meant to move us along the developmental path we were designed to move along. Real growth could not happen without the tension that forms the core of the pattern of transformation.

This pattern mirrors the natural cycles of nature; its core is: *birth /death / rebirth* or *beginning /muddle / resolution*. It is built into traditional rites of passage, the world's myths, and all sacred stories. This clearly recognizable pattern has played out across humanity's history as part of an ongoing repetition of cycles.

Transformation is the nature of life. The nature of transformation is *destruction* (breaking down) followed by *construction* (building up), or *disintegration* followed by *integration*. Change and transformation on the physical plane is ongoing, built in to our make-up, and inherent to life on both the personal and collective levels.

Transformation is how we access the higher levels of human consciousness, and the hidden mysteries of life. It is the way we satisfy the insatiable hunger in our souls that draws us ever closer to an eternal realm.

The process of transformation is key to social progress; it is necessary for growth and evolution. Adversity is necessary for progress and transcending duality. Unity is the result of the conscious confrontation of opposing forces, signaling the completion of the process of transformation.

The nature of transformation, as sacred scriptures, myth, ritual, and psychology agree, is to provide difficulties that are meant to be overcome and resolved, because this is what leads us back to wholeness and a deeper unity.

Trials and tribulations have a purpose; they are a bounty of divine bestowal. When tested to our limits, we can push beyond these and restore the dualities of life to their wholeness.

Opposition creates opportunity, maintains the law of balance, and is necessary for ensuring progress within an overall unfolding process. This same pattern of transformation is carried out on both the individual and collective level, for humanity just as for each person.

The key to transformation is a quantum-leap shift in consciousness that enables us to see that things aren't simply separate or opposite but are rather necessary parts of the same whole. This sense of wholeness, oneness, and unity is what makes their contradictions complementary, allows for a merging of opposites, and completes the process of transformation—which becomes a matter of uniting the polarities.

The goal of the transformation process is not the uncertainty or chaos that initially arises from the adversity, but the synthesis and union of seemingly separate parts, as they are merged into one whole. This is an essential oppositional process that makes up a sacred pattern found worldwide.

Far from being an accident, transformation is essential to ongoing progress. The *law of opposition* is key to understanding the process of transformation. As Jung puts it, "There is no balance, no system of self-regulation, without opposition... Nothing so promotes the growth of consciousness as this inner confrontation of opposites."

From a holistic perspective, opposites are not divided, they are complementary to each other, essential interdependent components of the same whole. Though reality is both One and many, its opposites serve the regulative function of maintaining the unity of the whole. As Heraclitus said, "The way up and the way down are one and the same." The meaning is in the whole, not its parts, as the One is made up of all things and all things come from the One.

Because we live in a dualistic world, the process of merging the opposites through transformation is necessary in our lives to complete our journey of living into wholeness. The way to wholeness is clear but not easy.

Carl Jung, who clarifies this further in his individuation process, sets the tone and the context for us, noting especially the difficulties:

> *The right way to wholeness is made up, unfortunately, of fateful detours and wrong turnings. It is a longissima via (longest way), not straight but snake-like, a path that unites the opposites... a path whose labyrinthine twists and turns are not lacking in terrors... [where] we meet up with those experiences which are said to be "inaccessible." Their inaccessibility really consists in the fact that they cost us an enormous amount of effort: they demand the very thing we most fear, namely the "wholeness" which we talk about so glibly and which lends itself to endless theorizing, though in actual life we give it the widest possible berth.*

This necessary terrain, with its "fateful detours," and "twists and turns," leads us to and through the understanding that opposition and adversity could not be more meaningful in uniting the opposites they magnify.

A systems view, or a holistic perspective, enables us to see all things as a whole first. This is most helpful in understanding how and why the flow of both evolution and consciousness function the way they do as components of a larger whole.

Because all things are tied together, they operate as a whole, rather than as separate, competing entities. This could lessen the "enormous amount of effort" required when we see our difficulties as separate from what we perceive as best for us.

The transformation taking place in the journey to wholeness involves a two-fold process of purging and reshaping everything we know for the wholeness of each person and the entire human race to be recognized and our unity established.

We are at the end of one cycle and the beginning of another, as Archbishop Desmond Tutu noted, "The atomized homogenous groups that existed in the past are no longer the truth of our world... We must recognize that we are part of one group, one family—the human family. Our survival depends on it."

When we privilege any of the parts above the good of the whole, this creates a response to everything based on separation and competition, which forces us to live by principles that exclude, where we approach everything with fear and bias, leading further to discord and prejudice overtaking our lives.

The work needed now, focusing on the whole first, creates a foundation based on harmony and cooperation. This foundation is built upon living by principles that unite, where we see all things as tied together in one reality. With this holistic vision, gazing out far enough, we can see a future leading to peace on earth.

With a consciousness of wholeness, we transcend the illusion of separation and transform our relationship to reality. This is the natural culmination of where the evolutionary impulse has been leading us. We are living into a new story, which tells of the birth of a new global community living in harmony with each other.

A consciousness of duality places separation above all else; a consciousness of wholeness places unity above all else. The forces of evolution are moving ever toward wholeness, though there are detours along the way.

A consciousness of wholeness acknowledges our sustaining strength to be in our diversity of views and appearances. Understanding this unitive nature of all things, incorporating this into our own deeper nature, and acting in everything we do as though this is what matters most, without denying any part of the whole their contributions to the whole, is how we become one human family.

There are safeguards within the evolutionary impulse that have already guided us along a trajectory through the ever-widening circles of unity from the family to the community to the city-state to the nation on our way back to wholeness.

We are now at the threshold of world unity. The promise of world peace has been with us for millennia. A glimmer of the light at the end of the Dark Night is beginning to appear. With our eyes focused on this coming dawn, our conscious activism moves us ever closer to the realization of the vision of the ages.

The eventual result of this imminent birth process, of our return to wholeness, will be, as Ervin Laszlo describes it, "a consciousness that recognizes our connections to each other and to the cosmos... a consciousness of connectedness and memory... [that] conveys a sense of belonging, ultimately, of oneness... a wellspring of empathy with nature and solidarity among people."

People endowed with this "planetary consciousness" will recognize their "role in the evolutionary process" and act "responsibly in light of this perception," as they know and feel "the vital interdependence of and essential oneness of humankind, and the conscious adoption of the ethics and the ethos that this entails," Laszlo says.

This is the organic process of evolution unfolding around us, with more and more people undertaking the journey to wholeness, embracing world-transforming trends, and activating this understanding in the world.

This mystery of oneness is at the heart of Creation. All things, counter-balancing parts of the same unified whole, are energized and held together by the same force throughout the universe. This connective, creative energy, known as Love, the divine spirit, or Grace, is the unifying force expressed in every dimension of reality.

Wholeness, and its inherent unity, is the underlying principle defining reality. Living into this wholeness is vital. Becoming familiar with the pattern of this story of wholeness is the next step.

Part Two

Pattern — Finding Connection in Apparent Randomness

The upheaval of our world
and the upheaval in consciousness is one and the same
We are only at the threshold of a new spiritual epoch.

—Carl Jung

4 Call to Wholeness

When fate arrives at your door,
there is no lock strong enough to hold it back...
Destiny does not wait for your mood to change.
—Anodea Judith

There comes a time in our lives when we are ready—or when we are given just the right nudge we need—to let go of what we thought we needed to hold to. This is when we are guided by some mysterious force toward a move we may not have anticipated. This moment of choice, or chance, comes when needed, no matter what it feels like is being interrupted, surrendered, or left behind.

Whether we've noticed it or not, something hasn't been fitting quite right in the big picture of our lives. There is some uneasiness or something uncomfortable, felt or not, about where we are, what we are doing, or where we seem to be headed. Something else, something more is needed in the way we are living our lives. It is time to take a step into the unknown, and onto the path forward.

This is the beginning of waking up, of becoming aware of something beyond what we've known. Far from realizing it at the time, we are whisked into a journey toward a higher consciousness. Yet it takes us even longer to recognize that this is destiny unfolding, taking us toward an innate, infinite potential we haven't yet glimpsed.

The call to wholeness, one of the oldest, most universal of all archetypes, sets us off on a journey we did not yet know existed. This is a journey to bring us into full consciousness of who and what we are.

This journey signals not only the beginning of a new life, the awakening of the self, or even the beginning of a process of transformation, but also an all-consuming, internal quest for truth, for understanding reality itself, and for reclaiming our wholeness that slipped away sometime after birth.

This is all part of our normal developmental journey needed to lift us beyond the realm of separation, to transfer our spiritual center of gravity from what is already known to what is as yet unknown, to re-unite us with all things and to restore our wholeness.

We enter a region of both treasure and danger, with a profoundly fluid flow of temptations and delights, without which we would remain separate, disconnected, unfulfilled, and unaware.

Not long after we embark on this journey, we realize that letting go was necessary for whatever does come next, which we could never have envisioned. Whatever we left behind soon becomes what wasn't really needed anyway.

This call to wholeness takes us to a different place or state of being. From home, from a relationship, from an unsatisfying career, from a serious illness, this call takes us ultimately to a new way of being or seeing things.

When we pick up this call, we loosen our hold on the bonds of everyday life to set forth on a series of experiences that take us into another world, a world where all is new, and everything is a teacher.

We become conscious of that part of ourselves that is part of everyone. We pass beyond the gate of limits into a land of wonder where boundaries cease to exist. We learn to listen as if each sound were made just for us to hear and understand. We feel the life in each moment as it comes to us.

We come to know that something more meaningful than we had ever known is imminent, as long as we remain open to life's mysteries and seek the meaning that makes the whole greater than any of its parts.

We learn that uncovering the secrets within ourselves is just as important as solving those outside of us. Everything we learn reveals the beginning of something more to be learned.

As we open our eyes to the moment, and grasp the wonder of its existence, everything, big and small, becomes a clue, each important in its own way. Everything we need to know is unfolding around us, especially in the beauty and order of nature where divine lessons are revealed with every season.

Our curiosity leads us deeper and deeper into what matters most, toward that which connects our own spirit with all others.

We find the usefulness of the universal in conscious relationship with others.

We have chosen to make decisions that will determine our destiny, as we strive, each day, to bring forth our inner virtues. This leads us to our own divinity, to knowing our own spiritual nature, as we live into our deepest calling.

We transcend our own seeming limits by seeing beyond the seen and understanding beyond the understood. We expand and evolve our consciousness as greater and greater levels of awareness and comprehension of self, society, the mysteries of life, and the wonders of the universe are explored in their fullest.

The independent investigation of reality unleashes our fullest potential and leads to the spiritualization of our consciousness. This awakening of inner capacities brings with it the recognition of new responsibilities for contributing to the collective wellbeing of all, which will reshape and restructure society.

This awakening has the power and the import to become a quest that nothing could deter us from. To seek to know reality, what is beyond what we already know, is to be open to connecting with something greater than ourselves.

Framing all myths, fairy tales, and sacred stories—and central to our own purpose, to who we are as human beings—is heeding this call, which becomes a search for truth initiating a pattern signaling that something of significance is about to happen.

In classic mythology, the archetype of the Call means leaving one place for another or leaving behind one status of being for another. This can take the form of entering a dark forest, an underground kingdom, or in the case of King Arthur and the

Knights of the Roundtable, going off on a literal quest to find the Holy Grail. In the fairy tale "The Frog Prince," passing a babbling brook becomes the scene and source of a dramatic transformation to follow, ensuring that the carrier of destiny has arrived.

Numerous contemporary forms of this archetype exist. It could mean ending one phase of life and beginning another. It could be precipitated by moving to a new area, a divorce, beginning a new relationship, becoming pregnant, beginning college, beginning a career, becoming seriously ill, all of which could result in a new way of seeing things.

In the Twelve Step programs, the call could be accepting our powerlessness over our own situation and beginning the process of recovery (Step 1).

Any of these contemporary forms of the Call could lead to the beginning of the awakening of the self, toward personal transformation. It is a release from some restrictive circumstance, enabling us to let go of what might be holding us back.

This time of encountering the unknown can create an atmosphere of irresistible fascination or curiosity. Most importantly, the call to wholeness summons us to a new spiritual or meaning-focused life.

A call to wholeness often comes when we least expect it. Sometimes it could come when we are not ready to begin something new in our life. If we cannot break loose of what we are doing, we may even refuse the call.

This would mean our status quo is too strong to give up. We may even need to be rescued from our complacency to be able to accept our call. We could also accept the call, step back, reconsider, and decide to refuse it again. Our call to wholeness may be foreclosed if we are too attached to our present status.

As soon as we do accept our call, we enter an archetypal realm in which everything is new to us. Some of those things that are new may first be perceived as antagonistic or even as enemies, as we have no idea yet who or what to trust.

But we do begin to sense that we are never alone, as we experience being assisted in some way when we need it most. This aid always seems to be from a protective figure, someone that is in the right place at the right time, to help us through an impasse. This assures us that we are under the protective hand of destiny.

In traditional literature, this aid usually comes in the form of a supernatural helper, a power animal, or a wise elder. In all cases, the assistance brings a sensation and assurance that we are being inwardly guided, and even a promise that the contentment of wholeness will not be lost. A feeling of being carried along toward some as yet unknown end, which nothing or no one can prevent, may also begin to become evident.

Today's versions of this aid may come from close friends, counselors or therapists, mentors, doctors or healers, teachers, a book we read, or even from the forces of the universe that seem to be working with us.

Receiving this assistance is the sign we get that we are on the right path. It is believing in "a Power greater than ourselves" (Twelve Steps, #2). On an inner level, this is when we are working in harmony with the forces of our unconscious and receive what mystics might refer to as "grace" or a divinely given blessing.

Next, crossing a new threshold, we begin to become more aware of new and different challenges than we've had before. Even though we feel inwardly guided, all is not clear sailing. The balance begins to shift again, and things get a little rough. We pass deeper into new territory (external or internal), and formidable powers pop up.

We may get a warning of an impending danger, as we look beyond where we are and into the darkness of what might lie ahead for us. We may even face a test of courage. Yet this is but the first guard we face in testing our commitment to what we have begun. Our goal is not going to come easily.

Contemporary versions of this motif include any experience that gives us a new level of challenges to deal with, such as doing something for the first time, raising children, getting a promotion at work, taking on more responsibilities, further academic pursuits, struggles in a marriage, or anything that causes fear of what lies ahead.

This motif means we need to summon our courage and advance toward the danger. This is our first test of faith, allowing us "to turn our will and our lives over to the care of the God of our understanding" (Twelve Steps, #3). As we make the effort to advance toward the obstacles in our path, we discover that the impending difficulty fades away as we proceed.

The final marker, or motif, in this first phase of living into wholeness is that of retreat. After a barrage of new challenges in a new realm, we feel a need to step back, withdraw, turn inward, reassess and reconsider things, take care of ourselves, cut ourselves off from the world and make further preparations for whatever lies ahead of us.

This retreat could be conscious or unconscious, chosen or forced upon us, but we quickly recognize it as a time to reassess where we are and where we may be going, and to do the serious work of looking inward, which ultimately leads to our renewal.

The classic example of this motif is Jonah entering the belly of the whale. This wasn't a planned withdrawal, but it was just what he needed. He was literally cut off from the familiar world, and unknowingly entered a tunnel that led to his rebirth.

There may even be threshold guardians at the entrance of this retreat to prevent easy access to anyone incapable of encountering the higher silences within.

In withdrawing, we shed the old, no longer useful or meaningful ways, and begin to seriously turn inward to prepare for self-renewal. Modern day versions of this might include entering therapy, living alone, being laid up with an illness, shutting ourselves off from others, going on a planned retreat, or even being locked down in a pandemic. This would also be the time during which we make a "searching and fearless moral inventory of ourselves" (Twelve Steps, #4).

All the classic myths, fairy tales, and sacred stories begin with this call, from Odysseus, Gilgamesh, Inanna, Icarus, Daphne, Moses, King Arthur, to Sleeping Beauty, Siddhartha and countless others. It takes them through an ageless pattern designed to fulfill our potential and carry us to our destiny.

Joseph Campbell said, "Myth is the secret opening through which the inexhaustible energies of the cosmos pour into human cultural manifestation." All forms of creativity, and even scientific discoveries, boil up from the magic realm of myth. Paralleling Jung's idea of the collective unconscious, Campbell is referring to the images sent up by the unconscious into the mind, where they become conscious thoughts and experiences that transform our view of ourselves in the world.

The universal archetypes that myth and ritual are built upon supply the symbols that carry the human spirit forward. What sets us off toward this transformative experience is a detachment from the world we have become used to and a growing ability to battle past our own personal and local limitations.

The archetypal call is a herald to a new and momentous undertaking, the dawn of an illumination, raising the curtain on the mystery of transformation, and rendering the familiar life horizon insufficient.

An irresistible fascination sets in under the spell of the unfolding mysteries. We become intrigued and drawn in further by those who appear suddenly at just the right moment bearing assistance or guidance, and all the other circumstances that are assuredly timed perfectly.

Evelyn Underhill explains "the mystic way" as a path we can take to realize our inner potentialities through a process of spiritual transformation leading to union (wholeness). The first of five states making up this journey is awakening into a transcendental consciousness that takes us beyond this physical world.

In refusing to be satisfied with someone else's experience, we are given our first direct experience of the Infinite, which is accompanied by feelings of joy and a sense of the divine in the world.

This involves the movement of consciousness from the individual level to higher, broader, more inclusive levels of reality, which can also bring with it a pendulum of emotions, from joy to pain, as St. Augustine describes: "I was swept up to Thee by Thy Beauty and torn away from Thee by my own weight."

The process of adjusting and adapting to all things new is primarily a matter of uniting a divided state of being, involving a steady remaking of character in relationship to the new reality being experienced.

By following the call to wholeness, we come to the boundary of the psychological realm and enter the spiritual-mystical realm of optimal development. It is in this liminal zone that we begin to learn much from the unfolding of nature around us and all other interactions, while opening ourselves up to peak experiences at the same time.

The mystic awakening, whether we feel ready or not, takes us into the life of the spirit in which we become a bridge for a never to be ended give-and-take between ourselves and the Absolute, where we know ourselves to be cousins of the stars above.

Within this mystic tradition, Bahá'u'lláh's *The Seven Valleys*, a path seen as the journey of the soul toward the object of its being, begins by aligning us with natural law and leads us toward a deep sense of social commitment, or sacred activism, of making a personal contribution to an ever-advancing civilization.

First is the *valley of search*, where we leave behind all selfish desires, become detached from all earthly things, learn patience and perseverance, and purge our heart of blind imitations so the truth of reality can be discovered.

This is a high standard for a search, such that "at every step, aid from the invisible Realm" is present, and as the intensity of the search grows, whoever seeks out a thing and persists "with zeal shall find it." This is how the awakening of consciousness is fulfilled, like a seed growing to fruition.

Rumi's "Be Lost in the Call" is another standard for this level of search:

> *Spirit, find your way, in seeking lowness like a stream.*
> *Reason, tread the path of selflessness into eternity.*
> *Remember God so much that you are forgotten.*
> *Let the caller and the called disappear;*
> *be lost in the Call.*

All who have undertaken this call to wholeness, who seek something beyond, have one passion in common, according to Evelyn Underhill: pursuing a spiritual quest to find a "way out" or a "way back" to what will "satisfy their craving for absolute truth," which constitutes the whole meaning of life, and leads to a unitive consciousness that includes a vision of divinity in all things.

This call to wholeness, or awakening, leading to a life of lasting change, and an intense, deeply satisfying search, also identifies the theme of many classic folk-rock songs, such as

"Urge for Going" by Joni Mitchell, "Highway in the Wind" by Arlo Guthrie, "Miles from Nowhere" by Cat Stevens, "Way Over Yonder" by Carole King, "Dawning is the Day" by the Moody Blues, and many others. Perhaps you've been called to wholeness by other styles of music or art forms. It is a ubiquitous theme that appears across traditions, generations, and cultures.

As Joseph Campbell assures us, we are not alone in this journey, there are myriad others who have gone before us:

> *The labyrinth is thoroughly known; we only have to follow the thread of the hero-path... where we had thought to find an abomination, we shall find a god; where we had had thought to slay another, we shall slay ourselves; where we had thought to travel outward, we shall come to the center of our own existence.*

With the faith needed to resolve these paradoxes, we shall end up with all the world embracing us and us embracing all the world.

5 Path of Purification

When we finally come to our knees...
We might realize that we are one people inhabiting one
country—
that we are all part of One Soul.
That we do belong. That we are all part of one cosmos.
—Marion Woodman

As we progress further into the journey to wholeness, going deeper into all that we encounter, we find everything more meaningful than ever before, we recognize a reason for our personal tests, and we become aware of our consciousness expanding toward the interconnectedness of all things.

We begin to see that we are in the right place at the right time, that time itself is more expansive than it has ever been, and that we are moving in the direction we need to be going, gaining an occasional glimpse of what is to come.

We know the inherent promise of our life, having resolved some initial but significant conflicts, though we have little idea yet where it is leading us. We do recognize, though, more instances of guidance and assistance coming our way, and we discover more of our hidden abilities and our innate potentialities.

Yet, at the same time, we become aware of those "fateful detours" Jung warns about as the challenges we face feel insurmountable at times. The path of purification is where things are the toughest they've ever been.

After our retreat, we are revived and strengthened enough to be better prepared for the difficulties we are about to encounter, as many new roadblocks, trials, and even those who would add to the divisions already in our way, quickly appear. This is a time, even after already having resolved some conflicts, when greater difficulty and cleansing comes our way, through which we discover unknown capacities that we are carrying.

Carl Jung's individuation process, a roadmap of our journey to wholeness taking us through many difficulties, focuses on a process of transformation, of what is needed to arrive at our essence. Individuation is a process on both the personal and collective levels of the unconscious being brought into full consciousness, resulting in a sense of the wholeness of the self and all existence.

Though the way to wholeness is long, requiring great effort, and made up of detours, twists, and turns, it is where we meet with experiences thought to be inaccessible but through which we find what is necessary to unite the opposites we encounter in the world.

Going through this Dark Night of the Soul reveals to us that our journey is becoming more about stepping up to new and more formidable challenges whenever they arise.

As we meet and overcome new challenges, we develop a consciousness detached from the world and its entanglements. We also meet those who provide assistance in ways we never anticipated. All are equal in their role as forces and manifestations of dark and light, and all bring to light more of our own hidden capacities.

We understand, from experience now, that transformation is necessary for growth, and that adversity and opposition are necessary for transformation. We have already seen how we are built to confront and overcome difficulties and challenges.

Though we live in the realm of dualities, our consciousness of wholeness is growing stronger. From our tests and temptations, our personal values and standards are becoming clearer and solidified, as the illusion of separation is being replaced by a certitude of a greater wholeness.

Our own path is showing us that trials and tribulations have a purpose in moving us along to where we are meant to be going. We are learning that out of crisis comes the opportunity to restore the seeming dualities of life to their reality of wholeness.

We are becoming conscious of having a natural need to be tempered, toughened, and sometimes restrained in our approach to all things. We know we have been undergoing a process of purification, that this will continue, and that this is necessary for our return to wholeness.

We have learned that we can push beyond our own perceived limits, dig deeper into our unknown inner realms, and facilitate our own process of transformation.

Our fear of letting go of the old way of seeing things is dissolving, as we die to the old, limited self, and are renewed and reborn, more than we were, with a full consciousness of oneness.

This is all unfolding from within, as we follow the natural inclinations of our developmental path designed to maintain the law of balance in the universe.

We recognize all that comes to us as needed for ensuring progress within a seemingly oppositional process, as our unique capacity of consciousness allows us to merge opposites and restore dualities to their hidden whole.

As the division between body, mind, and spirit is united, our transformation process, started long ago, nears completion, as our growth and continued evolution of consciousness is well on its way.

This is a time when the first signs of the fresh buds of a spiritual springtime appear, when a new life force is felt growing within us.

We may even be reminded by an inner voice to be loving, gentle, and respectful in all circumstances and toward all that we encounter from here forward, as love is the mystery that unites all opposites.

We recognize now that our task is to live lovingly, greet all that comes our way with grateful appreciation and deep gratitude, and offer a steady hand to the circle of humanity.

In classic mythology, this phase, characterized by an intense period of greater challenges, is where we meet with various tests and difficult tasks meant to confirm and strengthen our resolve in pursuing the process we have started and overcoming those obstacles that appear before us in a landscape of symbolism.

In our modern world, however, our trials are more often inner struggles where we are forced to face all that lies within us, and to come to know the internal landscape of our psyche more than we had before. This is the heart of the transformation process.

The conquests and complicated external landscape of mythic heroes could also become metaphors of what we may be dealing with at the hands of those around us, who, appearing as wolves in sheep's clothing, impose their will upon us.

Whether what we experience are outward representations of our inner world or not, if there is no muddle, or struggle to deal with, there can be no resolution. As we are learning from our own experience, stories contain more than a beginning, middle, and end. They reflect a pattern meant to bring about transformation. More deeply, they consist of a beginning, a *muddle*, and a *resolution* all of which together complete the process.

Examples of this motif today might include: having to submerge or sacrifice our true aspirations, suffering with a life-threatening illness, experiences of abuse, or even self-abuse, tragic loss of a loved one, struggling over the conflict between personal beliefs and personal behavior, severe financial burdens, being expected to accomplish something without having the means to do it, not being able to find a job, doing difficult work in therapy, or any other personal struggle that eventually leads to our purification and being able to embrace all aspects of ourselves.

What helps this process considerably is not only understanding what lies within us, but also being able to accept all of what does happen to us. This may be the point at which, in the Twelve Step programs, we "admit to God, to ourselves, and to another human being, the exact nature of our wrongs" (Step 5). This helps us realize and utilize our hidden capabilities and brings us much closer to our own rebirth.

This perilous journey into the darkness of an inner spiritual labyrinth, the way through a thorough purification of the self, is how we are cleansed and humbled, as our interests become concentrated upon transcendent things, and our youthful images of our personal past are dissolved and transmuted.

With the passage through the gates of metamorphosis well under way, the next motif of this phase is further assistance. Here we may get a temporary preliminary glimpse of what we have sought in our deepest wishes, a sign of what is yet to come.

In myth, this is the meeting with the goddess who represents everything that has ever been sought, all in one perfect form, as well as all that can be known. In contemporary form, examples of this motif might again be support from others just when it is needed, a mentor appearing, digging deeper into our creative resources, the renewal of a relationship, new realizations of what we do have, or, on an inner level, hints of our fullest, deepest, most complete nature.

This can bring an expansion of consciousness, a picture of wholeness, a deeper connection with our spirit nature, and a brief meeting with our future self. It comes to us as a promise of what we might find after we are fully renewed.

Usually following this is the motif of temptation. To make sure we are deserving of, and ready for, what could lie ahead, we may encounter temptations of many forms. They often come to us at a weak moment, as something we may have been struggling with for a while and may keep coming back until we have mastered it.

This is but a symbolic, outward means of testing us not for physical prowess but for spiritual fortitude and the degree to which our consciousness has been amplified and made capable of taking on the responsibility we are being prepared for. As Joseph Campbell has made clear, "Every failure to cope with a life situation must be laid, in the end, to a restriction of consciousness."

Due to the influence of patriarchal thinking in Western culture, in the classic hero myth, it is most often the woman who is the temptress and the man who is the hero. In this setting, her irresistible beauty, charm, or lure is most often the final test of the hero. If he succumbs, an innocent delight may become an agony to the spirit. For the heroine, man is often the tempter. At this point in the journey of transformation it is the purity of soul that is uppermost in guiding anyone's every move.

In our contemporary world, we could be tempted by an affair, unethical conduct at work, substance abuse, or any number of the dysfunctional compulsions we are prone to these days in the material world. If we are well grounded in the spiritual awakening that is happening to us at this point, the temptation may make us "ready to have God remove all these defects of character," "our shortcomings," and to help us make "direct amends" to the people we have harmed (Twelve Steps, #6-10).

Another contemporary form of this motif is our tendency to want "instant gratification." Becoming aware of what we see as a need can grow and grow in our mind and end up getting all out of proportion. If we are thirsty, our thirst continues to grow and grow. All we want is something to satisfy our thirst. Our mind focuses on what it will be like to quench our thirst. We want it all right now. This is what temptations do to us.

But temptations come to us to help us put things in their proper perspective, and to learn, perhaps repeatedly, that life's bounties come a little at a time. Moving beyond temptations means giving up the idea of having it all and being content with whatever does come our way whenever it does.

Whatever the temptation, this is when our ideals and values are put to test in order to be made as clear as possible. Even when we are serious about examining our own lives on an on-going basis, temptations can reappear at any time. The purpose of this motif is to give us a greater depth of self-knowledge to be able to handle any and all temptations.

To stumble once in a while is part of the journey. Having taken that first step into the unknown sets us up right away for encountering challenges that will expand our courage into new realms. This is how we recognize the support that comes our way, that we are not alone, and that others before us have walked this path too.

Facing difficulty is an essential part of our quest. This is what gives us greater confidence and shows us what is to come. Even temptations contribute to our growth when we hold firmly to the values we have determined are ours.

All things change in time. The pain we feel or see around us does not last forever. A Dark Night is but a brush stroke from the morning light. Even the journey of the soul has obstacles in its path. Patience and fortitude are required to the very end.

The pattern of beginning, muddle, and resolution we are living out is to be lived fully, so transformation can be completed. Rather than becoming overwhelmed by, lost in, or even detached from the muddle—and mistaking this for our destiny—we can always turn our vision to the forces that are truly assisting us each step of the way.

Among the many hurdles, roadblocks, temptations, and diversions along the path of purification are those that can prematurely cut short this process of transformation by causing us to think we have finished our hard work on this path before we really have. In contemporary terms, psychotherapist John Welwood calls this a "spiritual bypass," a common pitfall that tends to reinforce the illusion of separation.

When we use spiritual ideas, beliefs, or practices to avoid facing uncomfortable real world issues, emotional wounds, unfinished developmental tasks, or deny the darkness within us, we shift the focus away from the whole and bypass deeper issues that need to be resolved.

This deprives us of knowing our full identity. Even our challenges are part of the whole. What we suppress stalls the evolutionary impulse. Nothing changes without acceptance. The natural flow of all things is toward wholeness.

In some cases, if temporary, a bypass could serve as another developmental stage ultimately strengthening our resolve to address the avoided issue later. But often spiritual bypass ends up preventing growth opportunities as they appear in our lives.

Bringing in the principle of "as above, so below," which is designed to ensure the good of the whole, what applies individually applies collectively. What is sidestepped by society will persist until it is fully addressed. This is especially relevant in dealing with current social justice issues. The longer we bypass addressing directly the deep, longstanding socially ingrained issue of racism, and all other forms of prejudice, the longer it will be until we experience the reality of the oneness of humanity, ultimately the overarching spiritual principle of our time and a prerequisite to peace on earth.

Bypassing our own healing not only alters the journey we are on, preventing us from arriving where we were headed, but also places us on a different path with a much different outcome. This part of the journey, especially, is about finishing the work on ourselves first, when that opportunity is right in front of us, so we can heal, integrate, and unify all parts of ourselves to complete our transformational process and reclaim our innate wholeness. Only then are we better prepared to help others when that opportunity comes in its own right timing.

There is a big difference between spiritual bypassing and consciously living into wholeness. Bypassing not only stops us short of the goal but also dramatically changes that goal. Living consciously in the moment is the way to wholeness. This not only gives us gratitude for everything we experience, but it also opens us to the unknown, enables us to accept, embrace, and dissolve the challenges, and helps us arrive at the goal of gaining a clear understanding of who we are at our deepest essence.

When we've lived this pattern in its entirety, we know this is an experience we want to share with others. The universal pattern we follow in this quest engages us in conscious storytelling and becomes our guide in a lifelong endeavor.

A clear sign that we are moving closer to our goal is the arrival of unexplainable sources of help or grace. We may think we're in a hopeless predicament when—often at the last moment—some form of aid or guidance comes from an unexpected place, giving us the means to carry on. It is then that we find a resolution to our muddle.

The despair we feel or see around us is transitory yet purposeful, like the muddles that come and go in our lives. They will take their course, here one moment then gone. Both happiness and sadness have their place in this world, but neither must consume us.

Sometimes, in the midst of our own muddle, especially in the deepest, darkest part of it, we may feel more alone than ever before. Yet, what this timeless, universal pattern tells us is that we are never alone.

Knowing that we are living through a pattern that is emerging from the depths of our unconscious, that is central to who we are and what we become, assures us that not only are we one of thousands of others who have lived through this pattern before us but also that they have left the guideposts we need to make our way through this predicament.

This most difficult part of the process is designed solely for leading us to the resolution that will fully transform us into the whole being we always are.

Remember that there are two reasons why you are never alone. First, whatever it is that is challenging you is a human experience; at its core it is universal. Second, the most fearful moment, the heart of the process, the very turning point, is when everything shifts from a feeling of being separate or being alone to a feeling of experiencing the wholeness, or oneness, of everything and everyone around us. This is what carries us along to the needed symbolic death and rebirth that completes the process of transformation and brings with it the awaiting resolution.

Everything is purposeful. The dynamic tension between opposites is necessary. Joy cannot exist without sorrow; they continually wrestle each other, neither wins forever.

The season of doubt is followed by the season of certainty. Yet even certainty can be subject to the return of doubt, until we recognize their complementary places in creating the greater unity of wholeness. It is our ongoing effort to become more conscious of this inherent oneness that is the greatest adventure we can know.

The final motif in this phase, after overcoming our temptations, is renewal and rebirth. In classic mythology, this motif begins with an atonement, big or small, so that there is no longer an estrangement impeding our progress toward rebirth.

This could come through conscious and regular prayer and meditation, or a strong desire to live in harmony with all (Twelve

Steps, #11). The mystery is grace hides in the formidable. Whatever becomes our greatest challenge is where our greatest opportunity lies; out of our biggest test can come our greatest victory.

Rebirth, in this symbolic sense, consists of letting go of the selfish ego through an initiatory experience reestablishing contact with the innate whole self. This ensures a strong foundation upon which threats lose their power and fears gradually vanish.

Above all, this renewal allows for the full release of our potential, and perhaps for the first time we are ready to take on the new role of guide in a very important situation, as we are filled with compassion for all living things, knowing that all is one.

This enables us to feel a strong sense of accomplishment and peacefulness, experience grace in a new and deeper way, and also understand that time and eternity are two aspects of the same nondual whole.

In both a mythic and modern sense, we are reborn as more than we were. Today, this can take the form of deep insights and progress in therapy, a greater degree of self-awareness than ever before, an "ah-ha" moment or a peak experience, new achievements or accomplishments, seeing things around us for the first time, or really knowing a peacefulness and calmness in our lives that we hadn't before.

The ultimate boon bestowed during this consummate awakening experience is always scaled to the needs and new role of the recipient, a personalized symbol of the life energy available to all yet specialized to the requirements of the particular case.

While remembering that at our moment of great triumph we are also at our most vulnerable, we are now more ready than ever to take control of our life, and most certain of our newly tested and confirmed consciousness of wholeness, which propels us forward to give our gift of this understanding to others.

In mystic terms, this phase of the journey takes in the states of: *purification*, a purging of imperfections, false desires, and thoughts not in harmony with the newly perceived reality, creating experiences of suffering and pain, all necessary for the remaking of the character; *illumination*, a lifting of the consciousness from a self-centered to a Creator-centered worldview, verifying a divine presence and bringing with it a greater level of energy, activity, and often creative expression; and the Dark Night of the Soul, a symbolic death leading to surrender and rebirth, usually involving great inner struggle, confusion, helpless, and loss resulting in a deeper purification, leading to a merging with the larger will.

For the mystic, this is a time of discomfort and conflict, in order to bring to light even more the falseness around us so this can be replaced by what is most true. Our transcendental consciousness begins to take the reins, forcing on the surface mind a vision of contrasts and its own shortcomings.

Once this higher vision is glimpsed, it tends to maintain a hold on us, as Suso indicates, "Teach me, my only joy, the way in which I may bear upon my body the marks of Thy Love," or as Rulman Merswin describes his experience, "swept away by the transports of Divine Love."

Yet to maintain this ecstasy requires perfecting the practice of detachment through self-simplification by casting away the false complications of temporal life and arriving at a poverty of the senses, desires, and will, leaving only the purity of the soul, which fully prepares us for the consciousness of the Absolute and an illumined vision of the entire Creation.

In Bahá'u'lláh's *The Seven Valleys*, this process of purification is described as traversing the *valley of love*, intensifying an all-consuming search such that all self-awareness, reason, and sense of guidance are lost. Opposites, such as joy and grief, pain and ecstasy, are experienced in succession, along with confusion and paradox, in order to move us into a deep and lasting love of truth.

Next, in the *valley of knowledge*, we come out of doubt into certitude, our inner eyes are opened, the doors of vain imaginings are shut, we recognize providence in all things, and Creation is seen in its perfect form, with justice as primary and grace as ever present. This valley is "the last plane of limitation," the extent of human intellectual capacity, beyond which only personal experience of the divine wholeness of all things can carry one further.

The path of purification, with its purging, inner struggles, temptations, crazy transformative love, and renewals, is seen in the best of classic folk-rock songs, too, from Laura Nyro's "Time and Love," to Bob Dylan's "Girl of the North Country," to James Taylor's "Something in the Way She Moves," and Carole King's "Tapestry."

With our fullest potential easily accessible now, we also understand that we are still quite vulnerable, as we get a clearer vision of our future, what our reconfirmed ideals, values, and goals are, what our new role may be, and what gives us the greatest inner peace, as we integrate all the accomplishments we've made on our journey.

We accept the bounty of our fullest, most complete nature, break free of our personal prejudices, maintain our compassion for all life, knowing that the beauty we see all around us is within us, too, and strive with all our capacity to maintain this deep sense of interconnectedness and oneness.

6 Return to Wholeness

Let your vision be world embracing...
Dedicate the precious days of your lives
to the betterment of the world.
—Bahá'u'lláh

With our return to wholeness, we know how our life's journey will be fulfilled. Our energy intensifies and we are more focused on sustaining the unitive consciousness we have become convinced of as the highest reality.

This is the consciousness that serves as a foundation for the desire to devote our lives to the betterment of the world. With this consciousness of wholeness comes the willingly accepted responsibility to support and contribute to this wholeness in any way we can.

Buoyed by the resolution of prior struggles, and by our experience of renewal from this, we encounter a new kind of test, the challenge of knowing what to do next and how to integrate all of this into our new lives.

We desire nothing more than accepting the deeper responsibility of giving back to others the bounty of the new understanding we have been given, to serve the evolutionary impulse and the good of the whole.

To do this, we must learn to survive the impact of the world we are returning to, while continuing to live in the wholeness we have discovered around us. Though potentially a greater sacrifice than we've experienced before, we know it is worth it. We also know finding an inner balance in our lives is necessary for maintaining the new perspective we have attained, and that we have something of value to freely share with others.

Assured by an ever-present grace, we maintain the confidence needed to merge our will with the greater will, knowing our every breath will express the poetry of our soul, coming forth through a channel of contemplative stillness.

With this grace also comes an invitation like no other, as Desmond Tutu speaks of: "God holds out an invitation to us—an invitation… to wholeness that leads to flourishing for all of us."

Accepting this invitation gives us the assurance that we are doing what matters most to us and will most benefit the world beyond us. We are reminded often that we are doing what we most passionately love, what is personally sacred to us, and connects us to all life.

We become more aware of all separation vanishing, as a deeper connection with all life grows. Our calling now is to valiant acts of service. All our endeavors become a prayer, carried out with the intent to increase the visibility of love in the world.

We adhere to our internal integrity, knowing whatever work we do becomes worship, contributing in some way to maintaining justice, harmony, and balance among the peoples of the world, bringing one soul into communion with another.

We continue to give gratitude for all things received, while giving up what we thought we needed and what is beyond our control. We continue to reflect deeply on the life-changing experiences we have had and welcome the opportunities that take us to places that seem to be waiting for us to arrive.

We are grateful for having come full circle, returning to where we began, yet with nothing the same as before. To our experiences have been added a depth of understanding, emerging from our soul, our traveling companion for the entire journey.

Having let each experience sink deep within, to become a vital part of us, and having found hidden dimensions even in the clear-cut, we see all our experiences as vital in recognizing how they all connect us to everyone else.

We have lived a timeless, universal pattern and now see with different eyes. We have found spirit, soul, and all things everlasting to be greater than all things transitory.

We see the whole before the part, the universal before the particular, and the perennial before the changing. We know that this view of life is available to all, and that every generation finds this in their own way.

This is a consciousness we can all evolve into. By drawing upon the wisdom of the ages that explain what is beyond our physical world, what the patterns are that uphold this transcendent reality, and seeing this through the lens of our own experience, we verify this lasting truth for ourselves. Our dreams parallel everyone else's dreams and converge as we share the gift we have been given. Our highest good becomes the greater good.

Our return to wholeness is facilitated by knowing consciously the struggle of having transcended temporal boundaries and remembering that we are always in the process of becoming, interdependent and interconnected with all others.

We seek to maintain a holistic view of reality, as we take on a wider, all-inclusive identity, and integrate many more all-human qualities, characteristics, and virtues into our thoughts and actions as we strive to live as the whole being we are intended to be.

From our new lofty overlook, after all we have experienced in our call to wholeness and on the path of purification, with its rebirth, our return to wholeness begins with crossing another threshold, the challenge of attempting to pass on our new understanding to others, knowing they may hear it or not.

This is the lesson of classic mythology. Even great teachers like the Buddha doubted they could communicate to others the experience of their enlightenment.

Today, we could experience this motif as either feeling more responsible to ourselves or our family than to others, feeling overwhelmed or insecure, or, even with obstacles thrown in our way, getting the support and encouragement we need from those closest to us.

Knowing that giving back something of what we have been given is all-important, we also understand that it doesn't have to be much, just what we have learned from our experience of transformation, what we are capable of from the depths of our being. The successful return is always an illustration of what is humanly possible.

With the harsh realities of the world evident, we step into its flow with our eyes wide open, ready to accept whatever may come our way.

It may feel as though we are living in two separate worlds now, the divine (where we received our boon) and the human world, slipping in and out of each as circumstances change around us, yet we also understand that the two worlds are one, different parts of the same whole, though they appear as night and day.

Others may seem oblivious to what we have found, but we learn to live our own lives and give to others at the same time. Maintaining a balance between the two worlds, and between our inner needs and our outer responsibility, is our ongoing challenge. Detachment is always a key to living in the world after our transformation.

We figure out the most appropriate means to pass on our particular gift to others. It may be through our work, another role in life, or some creative expression. The task of clearly communicating our message may be made more difficult if those we most want to reach have a very different experience than ours.

We know the importance of surrender once again, as we did at the beginning of the journey. We have become more familiar with the feeling of being guided along by invisible hands, as well as trusting in our own destiny and making our own efforts.

We are grateful for what we have been given, and for what we have experienced. We are not perfect, nor ever will be, but we have learned to let go of our personal limitations, characteristics, idiosyncrasies, and even our hopes to some degree.

When we give these up, we find something better to take their place, knowing that grace continually surrounds us. This helps us manage the disappointments of the world and maintain self-assurance in the face of it all.

The final motif of the journey is living in wholeness. Feeling as though we are the master of the two worlds, with the freedom to live consciously in both, we are content with our lot in life, knowing we are always where we need to be.

We know well now, as Thomas Merton asserted, "There is in all visible things… a hidden wholeness. This mysterious unity and integrity is wisdom, the mother of us all." This is the anchor, the underlying principle now guiding everything we envision and do.

We have set as our goal to reconcile our individual consciousness with the unitive consciousness. We know this is realized through the cultivation of authentic relationships, which is also the final step of the Twelve Step Programs - "we tried to carry this message" to others and "to practice these principles in all our affairs."

Living this motif means being always active, doing whatever our role in life calls for, and accepting our shortcomings along with our successes. We feel responsible only for our own actions, and contribute something of benefit to others, without expecting anything in return.

We strive to continue to grow spiritually and help others do the same. We also realize that the narrative of the whole experience gradually becomes more important than the facts contained within it.

The gist of the deeper story, of all lasting myths and unitive narratives, is that we, through our prolonged inner commitment and discipline, give up all attachment to our own limitations and to the finite manifestations of the world in order to live in the beauty and bounty of the everlasting realms, able to relax into whatever comes to pass. Detachment is our secret elixir.

In the mystic tradition, the consummation of the mystic way is union, the unitive life, or becoming one with the Absolute Life. Although we must live in the world, we know we are not of it.

Living in both worlds at the same time, both as one, constitutes the highest form possible of living in harmony with the wholeness of Creation. Duality is thus transformed into nonduality.

Inner and outer harmony empowers transcendent vitality, bringing forth great deeds. This represents the highest form of consciousness, the deepest, richest level of human development possible, and includes the ability to serve as an ambassador to the Infinite, and a mentor to others. This is that state of being both patient and agent; patient with the Infinite, and agent in the world. This is the "honor for which [humanity] has been made," Underhill says.

In Bahá'u'lláh's *The Seven Valleys*, the *valley of unity*, where "the veils of plurality" are pierced, and "the heaven of singleness" is entered, marks a significant transition between the first three and the last three valleys, a bridge between the temporal and eternal where "the mysteries of divine creation" are experienced.

The *valley of unity* is where we understand the Hadith of Muhammad, "knowledge is a single point, but the ignorant have multiplied it," with a consciousness that resolves what seems to be a paradox in the planes of limitation – that duality is real – and replaces it with the understanding that oneness can be the only reality.

Unity here refers to the subjective understanding of the divine unity of all things, where differences vanish, and all things become one. Though equivalent to the final state of union in the mystic way, the valley of unity is preparation for the remaining three valleys, which are the highest realms of the soul's development, where the soul, mind, and body function as one, as a fully integrated, whole being. From this point on, we look upon all things with the eye of wholeness.

The *valley of contentment* adds a sense of inner peace, which comes from an experiential understanding of the Creator's bounty and grace, where tensions and oppositions are more easily resolved, and sorrow more easily dissolved.

The *valley of wonderment* reveals "a myriad perfect wisdoms" in the created world, and results in heightened spiritual empowerment and abundance that is felt as a new kind of deep, appreciative, joyous love of all things.

Finally, in the *valley of true poverty and absolute nothingness*, we experience the greatest spiritual wealth possible, the fullest expression of all things as one, and the deepest understanding of what is humanly possible in this world.

The outcome of this journey through *The Seven Valleys* is that reality is now seen as only that which endures and is everlasting, or the deepest qualities of the human spirit, resulting in an altruistic love that is given back to the world in whatever form of service to humanity is possible.

The return to wholeness, with its obstacles, threshold-crossing, giving of our gift, and the freedom to live consciously, is also seen in the best of classic folk-rock songs, from the Moody Blues' "Balance," to Bob Dylan's "New Morning," to Joni Mitchell's "Circle Game," to Cat Stevens' "Morning Has Broken," to Carole King's "Beautiful," and John Lennon's "Imagine."

Having undertaken the journey to wholeness, we are now living expressions of the primordial images, or archetypes, that have been buried within the unconscious of all humanity throughout time.

We begin to see what it means to be awakened, tempered, and committed, living out the promise of the ages, guiding others to the vision within themselves, of living in the consciousness of wholeness.

We are becoming a reflection of the ideal we have sought after, a spark of the force of love we have been comforted by, an echo of the voice that has guided our own path toward the light, and a transmitter of destiny to others, constantly assisting the spirit of the age.

In our individual wholeness, we find new allies also living the principles, virtues, and values we have lived into, and this leads us all deeper into our collective wholeness.

Afterword

Wholeness Is What We Are

Deepak Chopra, MD

holeness has become a buzzword in many areas of life; holistic medicine, whole-foods nutrition, and the human potential movement, which aims to create a whole person rather than a separate, fragmented one.

We can choose between whole foods and processed foods, or between holistic and mainstream medicine, with its reliance on drugs and surgery. But when it comes to a whole person, this is somehow different. Becoming a whole person involves the most fundamental questions about what it means to be human.

The nature of human consciousness enables us to take any viewpoint we want toward our own existence. Each of us decides how to relate to reality. The first three chapters of this remarkable book—on the principles of evolution, consciousness, and wholeness—provide a much-needed context and foundation for understanding our essential human nature.

Modern society, though, teaches us to relate to reality through scientific, rational, logical means. Nature, including human nature, is thus quantified, measured, mined for data, and given rational explanations. In this view, the mind becomes the product of the brain, because brain activity can be measured and quantified.

But this does not allow for the validity of subjective experience, which everyone obviously has. Sensations, thoughts, insights, intuition, creative ideas, or spiritual experience, etc., that occur "in here" are a realm of human existence that cannot be turned into data or quantified.

This has resulted in a clash of worldviews that runs deeper than the topic of science versus religion. To choose either the outer, objective world or the inner, subjective realm, as dominant squanders any hope of achieving wholeness.

What is most needed is to stop assuming that the outer, objective world is the only reality. Ancient spiritual traditions see the outer world as a distraction, an illusion, for good reason. This is because anything you can count, weigh, calculate, or measure is part of an all-embracing illusion—to grasp this fact puts you on the threshold of "real" reality, which is wholeness.

First, it is necessary to understand *illusion* in the same way that a dream is an illusion. Understanding a few facts about light, a basic property of nature, may help in this analogy. Photons, the elementary particles of light, are invisible and have no brightness. Why color is perceived as it is cannot be explained; the color red has nothing to do with its frequency or wavelength. Visual images in your mind's eye cannot be explained by examining the brain. The brain's visual cortex has no pictures in it; it is totally dark and devoid of light.

What ties these facts together is consciousness. Your consciousness gives light its brightness and color, creates images in your mind's eye, and experiences the world as a theater of events in time and space. Data, fact-gathering, and mathematical formulas can't explain consciousness.

Getting past the world of science, mathematics, and technology as an illusion isn't easy. But if you delve deeply into the fabric of nature, the most basic level, the quantum field, is where "something comes out of nothing," as physicists call the process of creation. Ripples in the quantum field, arising from the vacuum state, are the basis of the universe. And that's an enormous clue to escaping the illusion.

Could the eminent British physicist Sir James Jeans be right that these ripples are products of consciousness? He said that the universe was beginning to look much more like a great thought than a great machine. However, science is unable to explain how consciousness came about, leaving a big apples-oranges gap.

To heal this separation, we have to go back to when consciousness created something out of nothing. At some point after this, two tracks emerged and separated as the objective and subjective domain. Human beings became extremely good at balancing the two. A physicist can measure Higgs boson particles and also fall in love. But this balancing act keeps wholeness from being realized. Both worlds, as long as they are separate, divide reality.

The "real" reality dawns when the illusion of separation is replaced with wholeness. Reality is wholeness, which is all there is beyond any kind of split or fragmentation. How do we get to this unified field?

Science hasn't been able to agree on a way out of this dilemma; has spirituality? For centuries, spirituality has declared that the cause of suffering is the separate self. Isolated and alone, we build our individual stories with no acknowledged connection to wholeness. We remain like islands, separate and unaware of the other islands we are deeply connected to, *unless and until* we exchange the subject-object split—the very thing that placed us in separation—for a new relationship with reality.

Everything keeping us from wholeness presupposes wholeness is a choice. It isn't. Wholeness is everything. It is the One, the All, or Brahman, as it was known in Vedic India. Being whole, it cannot be accepted or rejected. Neither can it be lost. Wholeness has no separations, no divisions, no "this and that," no "yes or no."

Wholeness is a choiceless awareness in which we experience ourselves as whole: as pure existence and pure consciousness. We still accomplish the things we ordinarily do in the world—go to work, meet deadlines, take the family on vacation. But our experience is seamless and unified.

My book, *Metahuman*, is devoted to escaping the illusions we live by and replacing these with wholeness. But the road to wholeness begins by knowing what's at stake: a complete shift in how we relate to reality.

J. Krishnamurti referred to this as the first and last freedom. The vision of wholeness gets you on the path, supports you along the way, and stays with you after you realize that you are whole. Wholeness, which is what you are, cannot depart from itself, lose itself, or come back to itself.

There is only the process of waking up to reality. From there, the possibility of higher existence opens us up completely to the deeper process of living into our story of wholeness.

This wonderful book provides the framework and the guideposts needed to traverse this terrain. Use all its insights and exercises to get you to where wholeness becomes all there is, to where this becomes so central to your nature that you will see all things as the wholeness they are.

Epilogue

A Call for Stories of Wholeness

Earth is still a gorgeous, intelligent, living planet…
Restoring her pure waters, rich soils, and clean air,
and protecting her remaining wild forests, prairies,
and living creatures
as we love and care for each other is the only
possible way forward.
—Elisabet Sahtouris

We all hold a vision embedded deep within our heart waiting to come forth. As this unfolds in its own time, we recognize our lives as divinely guided.

Taking that first step into the unknown enabled us to find our greatest support, to learn that we are not alone, that others before us have also walked our path, and that every place we have been, every thought, worry, and fear we have ever had, is already part of our collective experience.

Confronting the unknown with courage revealed to us a capacity greater than we thought we had. Facing difficulty gave us greater confidence. Experiencing success gave us a glimpse of what is to come. Even temptations contributed to our growth when we held firmly to the values we set for ourselves.

We have emerged from the cave of illusion into full consciousness of the true light in the transcendent world. Through it all, we have come to the most important realization of all, that the only difference that matters in this life is the difference between the temporal and the everlasting.

While all else around us is uncertain and inconsistent, only the Changeless remains constant and permanent. The heavens encircling the earth in a loving embrace reminds us often that mind and soul, one and all, are united in wholeness.

We all come from the same Source, and we are on a journey back to where we came from. The most sacred endeavors along our path are to love, to serve, and to remember where we came from and where we are going.

Sometimes it takes so little on our part to bring so much our way from the spiritual realm. And sometimes we expend so little in giving so much to others, yet this is how we become instruments of grace ourselves.

Wherever our calling has led us, whatever our deepest insight has revealed to us, we know that we have a purpose, a role to play, whether it is restoring Earth's pure waters, protecting her living creatures, or loving and caring deeply for each other in our own unique way, we have felt that call to action.

The length and breadth of the playing field we are all on at this time, and upon which we all act to carry out our unique role is made abundantly clear by Joseph Campbell in the context he knows best: "The only myth that is going to be worth thinking about in the immediate future is one that is talking about the planet... not the city, not these people, but the planet and everybody on it."

The brightest light is the one that passes from heart to heart. As a wave of love washing over all on earth, this light is awakening us all to a time of promise, a moment of destiny. Evolution takes us along the path toward the recognition of the oneness of all, and the holiness of all things.

Our own remarkable evolution of consciousness has led us to a deeper responsibility now stirring within us, awakening a new desire to fulfill not only our own lives but others as well in whatever ways we can.

We are all related in our common experience of the transcendent and in our shared journey to witness the unity of Creation. Even with all who have set the markers and signposts on this path before us, and with all those to come who may find our markings, are we also connected.

In this solidarity of the human family, the supernal accomplishment of one is the attainment of all, as we share freely, consciously, and joyously in whatever way we can the fruits of our journey with all others.

Though this path is becoming more well-trodden, each one of us that heeds the call to wholeness is a pioneer for all those yet to set off on this life and world-changing trek to the summit of consciousness.

Lifted to this lofty level, we continue our tireless work of compassionate action cultivating harmony, justice, and peace in everything we do in the world as we partner with a higher will to ease ever closer to our own wholeness and to that of the cosmos.

Not from a remote plane of being, separate from the pulse of humanity, but in the very midst of normal, everyday becoming, we seek to further our own interbeing, in deep relationship with others.

At the same time, we are seeing both the death of old worn-out ways and the birth of a new holistic order with unifying principles and systems to support it. This process as a whole is the most hopeful vision of our present and future there is.

For Ervin Laszlo, the key to global transformation leading to sustainability and prosperity is a recovery of our oneness. By this he means "realizing our connectedness to the whole web of life." This "must be universal," "must come from the inside," and "depends on the evolution of our consciousness." "Spontaneous, lived experience," or spiritual experience, he says, is one of the best ways to verify the reality of wholeness.

Our return to wholeness gives us a new home on the unity side of the consciousness continuum, leaving behind any interest in the duality side of the continuum, which we know leads only to bias, prejudice, oppression, racism, and war. Our desire is to live by the unifying principles of a consciousness of wholeness.

Wellbeing consists of the diverse organs of the human body functioning as one, in harmony. This balance is found within the whole of creation, too. Our task in nurturing the good of the whole is creating conditions in the garden of the world for the seeds of cooperation, equity, unity, and peace to fully blossom.

Only the fulfillment of the highest potential of the individual leads to these conditions for the betterment of the world. There is a balance underlying a system of justice that would bring forth unity in diversity, as well. Punitive justice causes further separation. Only a system of unitive justice connects all in harmony, understanding, and compassion.

Bringing the story of wholeness into being means assisting the process of individual and collective evolution toward the goal of peace. Rev. Michael Bernard Beckwith says, "peace is a quality within us," and that world peace is dependent upon tapping into that part of our brain which is loving by nature. This is done by entering what he calls "peace consciousness." He sees a new paradigm emerging "on an increasingly global scale" with wholeness at its center.

James O'Dea has seen that the long and convulsive collective evolutionary process culminating in peace is well on its way, with a "blossoming of citizen activism" to go along with our "increasing awareness of our interdependence." Building "a culture of peace comes from a whole-systems perspective, which sees all things as interconnected and influencing each other."

Capturing this spirit of the age, the Universal House of Justice, the international governing body of the Bahá'í world community, released a statement in 1985 saying:

> *The Great Peace towards which people of goodwill throughout the centuries have inclined their hearts, of which seers and poets for countless generations have expressed their vision, and for which from age to age*

the sacred scriptures of mankind have constantly held the promise, is now at long last within the reach of the nations... World peace is not only possible but inevitable. It is the next stage in the evolution of this planet.

Far from meaning we can sit back and watch this happen, this view honors the evolutionary impulse, acknowledges a purpose to these turbulent times, affirms the eventual outcome, renews hope, and—most significantly—raises a call to action.

How we realize this vision of the ages is dependent upon each of us. We must take on our responsibility as proactive midwives assisting this birthing process to bring about a gentle as possible rebirth of the planet.

The vision of "peace on earth" is the goal of evolutionary advancements in an inner and outer process consisting of many interrelated steps, each dependent upon the others, always unfolding toward unity on more inclusive levels.

We are now in the midst of a process guided by two interdependent wings. First, the evolution of a unitive consciousness, built upon the principle of the oneness of humanity and a set of unifying principles supporting this, is preparing individual hearts and minds. Second, the means for collective wellbeing through an equitable and just system of global organization to foster world unity is the foundation being built out upon which those fully conscious hearts and minds will construct a culture of peace.

The Universal House of Justice further identifies the source of this evolutionary impulse:

Ultimately, the power to transform the world is affected by love, love originating from the relationship with the divine, love ablaze among members of a community, love extended without restriction to every human being. This divine love is disseminated by enkindled souls through intimate conversations that create new susceptibilities in human hearts that can gradually take on a new form in keeping with the requirements of humanity's age of maturity.

This collective maturation depends upon us bringing it into reality. Only the loving action we take now will usher in a gentle, peaceful path to peace on Earth. Love is the sacred activism of our time, binding all hearts together.

Finding our own way to support this evolutionary process through compassionate action every day of our lives, applying the wisdom, practices, and tools we have acquired along our journey, is most vital now.

The work of the day, the action most needed to be taken by each of us, is work across boundaries, across differences. Any step that can be taken in our everyday interactions toward anyone different from us in any way is to remove barriers that have been put up between us by others.

Joining hands across differences is the sacred activism needed now. Taking this action will establish a sense of belonging to the community of the whole. This is love in action, the work of a generation that won't happen without us.

All the superficial, illusory boundaries and differences between us need to be consciously broken down, dismantled, and crossed so we can experience no separation between any of us, as human beings. We have been made for compassionate, altruistic loving relationships and interactions.

There is a creative force at work in our midst guiding us in this direction, reminding us of our common memory, making us aware that unitive narratives are needed to bring fresh vision to the global community and that these are all interconnected expressions of wholeness, as Jean Houston notes in her Foreword.

The one form of sacred activism that may go the farthest in healing the great divide between us is sharing our stories of wholeness. This deeply personal process spreads ripples throughout the collective, *connecting the human family, one story at a time.* This will build a community of conscious storytellers, move us closer to living with a consciousness of oneness, and bridge the chasm between separation and wholeness.

As greater numbers embrace an orientation of global citizenship, find a unity of purpose, and integrate this into all spheres of life, from interpersonal to cultural to economic affairs, a consciousness of wholeness will become the norm in the near future just as a consciousness of nationalism was in the past. Our unitive stories of love in action that we have yet to tell will break down barriers and inspire others.

*A Guide to Living and Writing
Our Story of Wholeness*

We stand now where two roads diverge...
The road we have long been traveling... ends in disaster.
The other fork of the road – the one less travelled by –
offers our last, our only chance
to reach a destination that assures the preservation of the earth.

—Rachel Carson

You Are the Story
and the Teller

All sorrows can be borne
If you tell a story about them.
—Isak Dinesen

We are all participants in the story of our time, a new story that will shape, define, and carry us into the future we now envision. We are all living this story every moment of our lives. In this *Guide*, I invite you into the empowering and fulfilling process of telling your own version of this new story, the story of our evolving consciousness. Everyone has a voice in narrating our wholeness.

It has always been this way. The timeless stories of all ages come to life through living our own lives fully and deliberately. Being conscious of living a transformative journey and telling others about it is conscious storytelling.

This is what we now need more of. Conscious storytelling will become a dominant form of storytelling as we revive the Hawaiian tradition of talk story, sharing and exchanging our experiences of what really matters in life, of passing on our collective wisdom.

As we become conscious of the wondrous wholeness all around us, we want to share this gift with others. Conscious storytelling is a two-part process of living into the consciousness of wholeness and telling others about it.

In whatever way it unfolds in our life experience, living into wholeness sneaks up on us and changes who we are and what our priorities are. Conscious storytelling is by nature recognizing an obligation to pass this understanding on to others in a way that is totally natural to us. Living and telling this archetypal story of our personal and collective wholeness is the act of conscious storytelling.

The heart of this *Guide* is a series of three reflective writing exercises for each of the three main parts to this transformational pattern. Each one is designed to identify the elements of the archetypal narrative we have lived in our return to wholeness, while putting these together in a pattern that brings order and meaning to our experiences. These will make it easy and fun to tell your own story in this timeless framework.

To help see how living into wholeness can organically unfold in our lives, here is a piece of my story, because it is more than just mine. I became aware of archetypal experiences emerging in my life when I was 24, though there had been other such universal moments of truth earlier that prepared me for this.

There was a reason I was drawn from an early age to the mysteries of a reality I could not yet begin to fathom. The consciousness of my soul far exceeded that of my mind. Regular walks in the woods near my home were special times putting me in touch with a living universe. There was something about the woods, the stream, the trees, and all of nature that sang of union and heralded a call to my soul.

The day I was born the streets filled with parades of celebration, my mother told me. Not for me, but for the first atomic bomb that turned a world at war into a nuclear village. I came to realize later that my life was a subtle quest to find an elusive peace, inner and outer.

At age nine, when my grandmother came to stay with us, she modeled for me the life of the spirit. I was fascinated by her daily devotion, reading from *The Bible* and *The Upper Room*. I didn't know it then, but she made a difference to my soul.

Around this time, sitting on my bed looking out the window, reflecting on my grandmother's faithfulness, a "voice" from within, or maybe from someplace else, came to me saying, "Someday *you* will know God." This propitious moment took its place as a subtle thread running below the surface of my life.

In college, majoring in philosophy, I realized the supreme force of the universe is the unknowable Essence, though the manifestations of its bounty are evident everywhere.

After a master's degree in folklore, my investigation of reality began in earnest. Philosophy, world religions, and mythology became my passion as their common core became more and more evident to me.

Then, the summer of 1969 called me into a wholeness I was not yet aware of, as a series of serendipitous experiences unfolded that seemed like they were waiting for me to arrive.

The right people came into my life at the right time, nature spoke to me in ways I hadn't heard before, and circumstances brought unimagined opportunities.

As a counselor at a summer camp, one July afternoon, all the campers and counselors gathered around a small TV to watch the moon walk live. Seeing the earth as never before, with no boundaries, just one planet with one human family on it, changed everything.

A couple weeks later, having been invited by Pete Seeger to sail on the maiden voyage of the Hudson River sloop *Clearwater* from New York to Albany, I listened as he shared his vision from a stage at South Street Seaport:

> *The idea is simple. We want people to come down to the river again… young and old, black and white, rich and poor, longhair and crewcut… You see, everything in this world is tied together. Once you clean up a river, you have to work on cleaning up society…*

With a new mentor who came along just in time, my evolving worldview solidified around knowing all things in the same whole *are* interconnected.

After a few sloop festivals along the way, the *Clearwater* arrived in Albany just in time for some of the crew to attend the Woodstock music festival, where some 400,000 of us *experienced* a community of wholeness.

That fall, living in a small cabin in the woods by the river, I deepened my study of the world's religions and further explored the cycles of nature in the woods around me, also visiting Arlo Guthrie at his farm in the Berkshires with Ramblin' Jack Elliot, one of the sloop singers I had sailed with.

Living as a guest in a nearby Franciscan monastery that winter, and on a visit to New York City one evening, while looking in the 8th Street Bookshop window, a book on mythology caught my eye.

Inside, after paging through the book for a while, I looked up at a poster on the bulletin board and discovered that Joseph Campbell, whose book I was reading, was giving a talk that same evening at Cooper Union, a few blocks away. With minutes to spare, I walked right over there.

Sitting front and center in the Great Hall, a huge crowd filed in all around me. I listened intently to every word he said. As if I were the only one in the hall, he described an ageless archetypal pattern, mirroring perfectly my own experiences at the time.

Afterwards, I introduced myself, and told him how much what he had to say meant to me. He responded very warmly and encouragingly. We kept in touch, and I visited him in his Greenwich Village home a few times. On one of those occasions, he gave me a signed copy of his book, *The Masks of God: Creative Mythology*, the final volume in a series in which he reflected that the series confirmed for him:

> *A thought I have long and faithfully entertained: of the unity of the human race, not only in its biology but also in its spiritual history which has everywhere unfolded*

in the manner of a single symphony, irresistibly advancing to a mighty climax.

He became a mentor helping me make further sense of the universal mythic pattern I was living. I had no idea listening to him demystify my journey that I would soon return to the college I graduated from three years earlier to teach a course on how the poetry of folk-rock lyrics followed the same timeless pattern. This is what all these experiences had been preparing me for, and I got to share with the students my lessons learned.

This period in my life was the fertile ground for what became *Year of Living Deeply: A Memoir of 1969*, chronicling a process of living into wholeness that connected me to the universal layer of my existence, a pattern countless others have lived, and a timeless story told by so many.

Through these experiences, with an openness to the mysteries that lead to a deeper understanding of ourselves and a deeper connection to others, I've learned that consciousness evolves with experience, but only through our own conscious integration of it all into a new understanding of reality.

As more and more of us are having experiences of the awakening of new capacities that give us a clearer picture of the whole, this is bringing with it the recognition of new responsibilities for a collective maturity that is restructuring society. Seeking our own investigation of reality and finding the truth that fits with the spirit of our time is more critical now than ever.

Living into wholeness takes us right into the sacred realm of life. It helps us explore those elements of life that make us authentically us. It gets us in touch with our soul, and everyone else at the same time.

Telling the story of our return to wholeness has a ring of "Once upon a time..." to it, focusing us on the timeless and universal elements we share with others. The process itself transports us to that place where we find a deep connection to other lives, and where past, present, and future merge.

As we become more familiar with the experiences, motifs, and emotions in our own lives that we also share with others, we recognize a deeper connection with others and a more profound appreciation for the resilience we all share as well.

Living and telling our new story connects our lives to those who have gone before us by conveying what is most important and meaningful to us, especially the ultimate concerns and beliefs that have directed our growth.

We can tell about our process of reclaiming our wholeness as a series of events or experiences connected by a common thread in any style we are comfortable with. In telling this story, we will gain access to our conscious voice, that part of ourselves that finds, understands, and expresses the deepest meaning in what we experience.

This is the voice of our soul, the voice that is in touch with our deepest values, beliefs, and aspirations, our most universally human experiences. This is the voice that communicates back and forth between our soul and our mind, carrying information about the lasting, eternal world for us to utilize in the everyday world.

Being aware of this exchange and nurturing this on-going communication with our conscious voice on a regular basis keeps us in touch with our higher consciousness, what Jung called the collective unconscious, where we connect with those innate aspects of ourselves that lead us toward wholeness.

Our own process of living into wholeness tells the story of how we have overcome formidable obstacles in our way. It includes symbolic expressions of having gone through a Dark Night of the Soul, or having traversed treacherous terrain, that need to be told in order to come to some new understanding of ourselves.

Consciously living and telling the story of our return to wholeness is a process of remembering and self-discovery that adds perspective, depth, and connectedness to our sense of being and solidifies our identity. This can be an extremely powerful and personally significant experience. It is not therapy, but it can be therapeutic. To tell about our life in this mode is to give our life an inner power that we all yearn for, that leads to a selfless desire to contribute something of our own to the good of the whole.

Keys to a
Timeless Pattern

Planetary consciousness is knowing, as well as feeling,
the vital interdependence and essential oneness of humankind.
It is the conscious adoption of the ethic and the ethos this entails.
—Ervin Laszlo

Living into wholeness follows a roadmap for navigating life's transitions while we undergo a transformation of character and personality. Its ageless, universal pattern guides us along an evolutionary trajectory toward a unitive consciousness.

The world's sacred stories, myths, and folk tales are built upon this pattern. Culture may vary regarding social customs and laws, but sacred tradition is remarkably uniform when it comes to the progress of the human spirit.

In the endless telling and retelling of sacred stories, the core pattern is always evident. And in the close examination of a life, that same pattern is evident as well.

Spiritual and mythological themes and motifs are not just buried in our unconscious mind. They are the essence of our waking moments as well. Experiencing archetypal themes in our conscious life is one of the purposes of life, because they are agents of change leading us to wholeness.

To live this pattern is to experience the total range of human life. The spiritual sense of the pattern is evident in the initiation rites of traditional societies, where the child is guided to leave behind its childishness and take on its adult responsibilities.

Most importantly, this process has changed who we are, our identity has shifted so much that we now know who we are at our essence. We have woken up to our true nature.

Living this pattern not only expresses a universal psychological process that we all have much to learn from, but it is also a spiritual experience that brings with it a new level of commitment and responsibility to others.

This pattern is thoroughly known, for there have always been myriad others that have gone before us, illustrating the pattern of spiritual renewal, which always involves a series of significant trials and ordeals leading to triumph and victory.

Most evident in initiation rites, they are never an easy experience. The importance of these personal ordeals should not be lost on us today. We see more and more now how horrendous sufferings and tests people have endured in their lives come to the surface and demand attention.

These sufferings are the reason for the emergence of the many Twelve Step programs, beginning with Alcoholics Anonymous in 1935. The way to both recovery and spiritual growth is through consciously letting go of the ego, embracing our pain and shortcomings, and releasing ourselves from their bondage with the help of a "higher power."

The process of acknowledging our condition and consciously striving to go beyond that to a new status mirrors what has happened forever in sacred, mythological realms, too. In all its various forms, this pattern carries within it a test of courage, which gives us the opportunity to summon from within what is necessary to achieve a transformation of consciousness.

The heart of traditional initiation rites, the mystic way, the individuation process, and Twelve Step programs is the alteration of inner awareness leading to a change in the way we perceive ourselves. This utilizes all our experiences to bring about a transition from one level to another that is both psychological and spiritual at the same time.

Living this sacred pattern, whether in a traditional ritual or in everyday life, is learning to see the positive values in what appear to be negative moments. We are often challenged and tested significantly, but rarely if ever beyond our capacity.

Successfully making it through the entire process of transformation happens by living at the upper range of human possibility that lies within us all.

Our response to the crucial, transformative moments in our lives determines everything that happens after that. Because this is a divinely inspired process, connecting us to the Changeless, to the sacred, it always awakens noble sentiments within us and spurs us on toward carrying out what we see as our highest purpose.

This process connects us to our deeper humanness, to what we have in common with all others, becoming a validation that we are all related. Acting upon this knowledge of who we really are and carrying it out the rest of our lives in everything we do fosters living in a sacred manner.

Here are a few things to remember in consciously living into the wholeness we are all born with, to ensure that we make the most of this opportunity.

Identify the experiences in our life that others before us have experienced. These moments of truth when the eternal breaks through into our daily lives are archetypal experiences emerging from the unconscious that set us off on a whole new direction in life. They create the framework that makes our lives timeless, universal, and sacred, while connecting us to all others. The more we become familiar with the timeless elements of stories and the sacred pattern they follow, the more we will understand and recognize those same elements in our own life. This shows us how we have moved from order to disorder and back to order in our lives.

Consciously acknowledge and embrace our experience of personal struggle. As we do this, we experience a symbolic "death" to what does not serve our evolving consciousness and enter into the grace of "rebirth." We can all know this firsthand, every time we recognize the renewing power of what gave us our greatest challenge.

Become fully conscious of the universality of the evolutionary trajectory our life journey follows in its struggles and transformations by recognizing the commonalities between the monomyth, the mystic way, initiation rites, and the individuation process. Each of these unitive paths mirror each other, as reviewed in chapters 4, 5, and 6, in guiding us through a process of letting go, being purified and transformed, and becoming whole and fully integrated into the world.

The essence of living into wholeness is a drama depicting challenge followed by assistance, or crisis followed by victory. This pattern being played out in our lives puts us in a position to discover and utilize our hidden capacities. As we do this, we rise to a new level of consciousness.

Opposites creating tension in our lives offer us the opportunity to summon from within what is necessary to merge these opposites into a new whole which at the same time achieves a transformation of consciousness. The real story is not the slaying of dragons out there, but of slaying dragons within us, for that is how we become whole, how we reach our fullest potential, and how we overcome our own challenges to achieve our potential.

Living into wholeness takes us right into the sacred realm of our life. It helps us explore those elements of our life that have made us who we are. It gets us in touch with our eternal essence and with everyone else at the same time. It opens us to the timelessness and universality of our story.

The emphasis here on the timeless and the universal aspects of our lives is warranted because every life consists of some conflict or problem to be resolved. Whatever our own trials look like, feel like, or do to us, their purpose is helping us regain a lost balance, recognize the oneness in duality, and anticipate a resolution during the challenge.

Identifying and highlighting those moments in our lives when opposition creates conflict, when joy and sorrow embrace, leads to a transformation that remakes us into someone we weren't before, and our lives become infinite. Our ongoing challenge is to remember to live in both worlds—the temporal and the eternal—at the same time.

As we've seen, the pattern of living into wholeness is made up of the three key archetypes of *Call, Purification,* and *Return,* or *beginning, muddle,* and *resolution.* These include an awakening of consciousness, an awareness of being guided, the beginning of transformation, approaching danger with courage, withdrawing and turning inward, utilizing our hidden capacities, expanding our consciousness, dying to the old, being reborn to the new, realizing a serenity and compassion, accepting both joy and sorrow, remaining assured, and doing what we can to restore the world to wholeness.

This pattern guides through the ordinary world and into what feels like a realm of wonders, where we encounter formidable challenges and emerge renewed, able to bestow a gift of some kind upon others.

It is a process of letting go of one status, acquiring a new status that expands our awareness and abilities, and then living in this new status with a greater impact on others. When we become conscious of this experience, we realize that we have returned to our innate state of wholeness.

Everything is laid out for us; it may be invisible, but it is there. The path has been illumined by prophets, seers, and mystics throughout time; it comes with instructions meant to guide us to and successfully across the thresholds in our lives where opposites meet, clash, and ultimately merge.

This guidance can now be seen as a blueprint designed to keep us on that path and bring about the transformations that will lead us to our destiny. (See the Blueprint for Living Our Story of Wholeness following the introduction.) Here are three practical steps to assist us in following this blueprint:

Remember who we are at our essence, where we have come from, what our essential nature is, and what we are doing here. This is how we will discover what our potential is, where our destiny lies, and where we are going. This is preparation for waking up, becoming aware of something beyond what we've known, and embarking on the quest for a higher consciousness.

Re-vision our entire life experience in the context of the timeless pattern that the process of living into wholeness follows. This is the beginning of recognizing how a larger will is unfolding around us and discovering how our own experience aligns with this. This is how we integrate our experience of the timeless pattern with our conscious knowledge of its meaning and purpose for our lives, which is what gives us the awareness of the evolutionary trajectory we are on.

Reclaim and embrace our own innate spiritual nature, even if we've been aware of it already and have been nurturing it, to experience even more now how this connects us to the collective spiritual heritage we all share. This is how we consciously merge the knowledge we've gained from our personal journey to wholeness, by integrating this into our daily lives and actions.

These three steps of remembering, re-visioning, and reclaiming, a whole process consisting of knowledge, volition, and action, will also help complete and solidify the transformations we have experienced in our lives, serving to keep us on track and closer to the Source of our being, while supporting our desire to share with others what we have found for ourselves.

Here are a few more practical keys to applying the fruits of living into wholeness and making more effective use of the Reflective Writing Exercises that follow:

Become more familiar with the three major parts of the Blueprint for Living Our Story of Wholeness. This pattern is ubiquitous to all narrative forms, including sacred stories, myth, ritual, folk tales, many developmental theories, and other transitions. The pattern as a whole provides a clear overview of the entire transformation process. It is important to be able recognize any phase of this pattern as it is happening in our lives. This can be done in earnest by studying any of the primary sources of transformational literature, starting with those in the further resources list. This will make the use of the exercises and worksheets that follow more natural.

Become more familiar with each motif within the three main parts of the blueprint. Each of the three major archetypal components of the blueprint have their own smaller elements. These are illustrated in detail in *The Hero with a Thousand Faces*. A summary of these smaller elements of each archetypal part is offered in the blueprint as well as the writing exercises. Understanding these smaller elements of the pattern will add more meaning to the whole and help identify those elements in our own experiences.

Reflect deeply on your own journey to identify the archetypes and motifs that have emerged in your own life experiences. All archetypal images are already contained in the collective unconscious of all of us and become conscious through living reflectively. Our experiences mirror the ageless archetypal experiences of those who have gone before us, making our own lives timeless, universal, and sacred.

Reflecting on and telling, or writing, our experience of the process also consists of three steps. Each of the three main parts of the Blueprint—Call to Wholeness, Path of Purification, and Return to Wholeness—comes with three exercises.

We will start out with the overview of each part from the Blueprint, to have the entire part in mind at the beginning. We will then go on to each of the three exercises for each part, which consist of:

The first exercise for each of the three main parts focuses on the key point for that part and then offers questions, or writing prompts, designed to help us recall specific events and experiences in our lives that mirror the archetype and motifs of that part.

The second exercise, in the form of a worksheet, provides examples of the archetypes and motifs from that part with blank lines beneath it where we can fill in our own personal motifs that we have experienced and what they mean to us in the broader context of our own life.

The third exercise for each major part serves as a guide to turning our rough notes from the first two exercises into a flowing narrative of the three parts, which will then be merged into one continuous narrative of the new story of our journey to wholeness.

When we put the three parts of our narrative from our notes into a whole, we have our own version of a timeless, universal, unitive narrative consisting of *beginning, muddle,* and *resolution,* or our own expression of living into wholeness built upon our own experience of it.

Within this framework, we have a sequence of events, experiences, and feelings in our lives that demarcate these from any other period in our lives, which spotlight how some kind of conflict or problem was resolved, a balance regained, and our wholeness was reclaimed and manifested in the world.

This pattern can be repeated many times in our lives. It may be most effective if a "first time" is chosen to focus on, since that will be when the pattern is freshest, fullest, and maybe means the most to us. But if that time doesn't feel significant enough for some reason, it could be as important to focus on the experience of this pattern that was most transformative. Whatever time is chosen to focus on here will be a "good story" in that it is timeless and universal, following the pattern designed to lead us back to wholeness.

Before moving on to the series of exercises that will bring us to our new narrative of returning to wholeness, take another close look at the Blueprint. After we have its flow and meaning clearer and fresh in our mind, reflect on these key questions as a final prep for facilitating working with the series of exercises.

- *How is your life unique? How is it universal?*
- *What has been your personal struggle or quest?*
- *What deep personal truth has this led you to?*
- *What do you most want others to know about your life?*
- *What is there about your life that will most connect with the lives of others?*

- *What understandings are most significant in looking at your life as a whole?*
- *How do you most want to be remembered by others?*

The answers to these questions can become the leaven of telling your new narrative.

The real key is remaining open to how the challenges of our life can be beneficial to others. Remembering these times in our lives of waking up, letting go, rising to new challenges, and embracing the wholeness we have always been, has contributed not only to our growth but also to the growth of those around us.

If we were to tell this as our sacred story, it would be one of who we are at our depths, through having overcome our challenges, achieved transformation, realized our potential, and become whole. This is what everyone can benefit from.

The personal benefits of telling our own unitive narrative are ever-expanding. Here are a few that can be kept in mind as your new story emerges:

- Deep reflection on our own experiences enhances, expands, and adds greater meaning to the experience itself and to our lives.
- Writing—giving real words to our thoughts—brings clarity, understanding, self-knowledge, and greater self-confidence.
- Telling our story brings it into a sharper focus and helps clarify our sense of personal identity.

- Telling our story can be a way of purging or releasing ourselves of certain burdens that we may not even be aware of until we let them go.
- When we share our story with others and it is understood and accepted, we will feel validated and valued.
- We can gain great joy, satisfaction, and inner peace in sharing our story with others.
- What may initially feel risky, in telling our truthful story, may end up becoming a very powerful part of our resolution, or return to wholeness, as it is for those in Twelve Step programs.
- A truthfully told story is what most connects us to others. Telling our story illustrates and makes real our inherent interconnectedness with others. It is how others see a reflection of themselves is us.
- Sharing our story triggers memories or an awareness in others of how similar our experiences are.
- A truthfully told story carries emotion that may make another laugh or even cry, which in turn impacts us similarly.
- Our stories are what tie us all together, as members of the human family, the storytelling species.
- We tell our stories because they are who we are; they are a vital tool for making us whole.

Take as much time now as needed to go thoughtfully and thoroughly through each of the following exercises—while referring often to the Blueprint for Living Our Story of Wholeness for its overview of the entire pattern—to tell your new story of wholeness for others to learn from.

Call to Wholeness Reflective Writing Exercise

Key Point

The call to wholeness, one of the earliest, most universal archetypes in the world, is not only about the beginning of a new life, the awakening of the self, an external journey of unfolding destiny, or even the beginning of a transformational undertaking; it also signals an internal quest for truth, for understanding reality itself, *and* the unleashing of our fullest potential.

Writing Prompts

1. Use this as a mantra to meditate upon ~
   - *Letting go is necessary for reaching out; retreat is preparation for emergence.*

2. Follow your path backward to those times in your life when something really changed for you. Think about each one as you come to it. Maybe one of these experiences

sticks out the most. Reflect on these questions about a time of great change:

3. Which new phase of my life has had the deepest, longest lasting effect on my life?
   - What did I leave behind? Did I know where I was headed?

4. Did I ever have the experience of being helped by someone or something, or being inwardly guided when I most needed it?
   - Who or what was it that was guiding me?

5. Have I ever felt like I had to summon all my courage to overcome a new or dangerous predicament?
   - What was it that was in my way at the time, that I had to overcome?
   - Did the danger seem to fade away as I faced it?

6. Was there ever a time when I just had to stop everything and turn inward?
   - Did it feel like I was cut off from the rest of the world?

7. The experiences you come up with for these questions are probably connected to each other as a series of events. Try to identify the common thread that links them. Write down your immediate thoughts to these questions in notes or a rough outline, then transfer them

to the parallel archetype or motif on the blank lines in the following Call to Wholeness Worksheet. Later, you can transform these notes into a flowing narrative.

Workspace for Call to Wholeness Reflective Writing Exercise

_____

_____

_____

_____

_____

_____

_____

_____

_____

_____

_____

_____

_____

_____

_____

Call to Wholeness Worksheet

ARCHETYPES & MOTIFS

Call to Wholeness

A new beginning; breaking a familiar pattern; leaving home; moving; divorce; getting married; becoming pregnant; starting a new career; a serious illness or loss, a new way of seeing things

Meaning

Waking up; entering the unknown; a journey to a higher consciousness; the beginning of transformation; setting off to fulfill one's potential; destiny unfolding

Personal Experience of the Archetype or Motif and its Personal Meaning

_____

_____

_____

_____

Assistance

Grace; aid from beyond; help from a friend, a therapist, a lawyer, a teacher, a doctor, a book, or from the universe

Meaning

A protective power appears; feeling inwardly guided; sensing we are never alone

Personal Experience of the Archetype or Motif and its Personal Meaning

_____

_____

_____

_____

_____

Initial Challenge

New struggles, fears, and tests arise

Meaning

Crossing a threshold; test of courage; danger fades as we advance

Personal Experience of the Archetype or Motif and its Personal Meaning

_____

_____

_____

_____

_____

_____

_____

Retreat

Going within; living alone; entering therapy; laid up with an illness

Meaning

Withdrawal; turning inward; taking care of ourselves; reassessment; cutting ourselves off from the world; a desire to develop ourselves more fully grows within us

Personal Experience of the Archetype or Motif and its Personal Meaning

_____

_____

_____

_____

_____

_____

Call to Wholeness – Shaping a Narrative

From Notes to Narrative – Part I

After the first two Call to Wholeness exercises are completed to our satisfaction, we can begin to take our notes from these and turn them into a flowing narrative that tells our new story of the initiating event that led us into unknown realms and a new phase of life.

The form and style we choose to tell our story is completely up to us. It may work best if it is whatever fits our experience. Feel free to be creative, imaginative, and open in expressing this experience as a story. We will want to tell about our journey in a style or genre that we are most comfortable with. It could be realistic, allegorical, impressionistic, or some combination thereof, remembering that what we are telling is our inner truth, that part of our life that most connects with the lives of others.

- Re-read the rough notes from the previous two exercises, our responses to the writing prompts and our own life events, experiences and what they mean to us, reflect on how these would best fit into a comfortable story form, and then turn them into a flowing narrative that includes all our experiences paralleling the first part of this timeless pattern. This may be where you'll want to take your rough hand-written notes and put them onto your word processing software.

- When our first draft is completed, take some more time to look this over, being sure that the essence of that entire experience is captured as clearly as possible, before going on to the Path of Purification part of the journey.

Path of Purification
Reflective Writing Exercise

Key Point

Transformation is necessary for growth; adversity and opposition are necessary for transformation. We are built to confront and overcome difficulties and challenges; trials and tribulations have a purpose. This process of purification is meant to help us restore the dualities of life to their inherent wholeness.

Writing Prompts

1. Use this as a mantra to meditate upon ~
    *   *Out of crisis comes opportunity; following purification is restoration of the whole.*

2. Coming out of part I, this *muddle* phase of your story reveals the inherent promise of your life, after having

resolved some significant conflicts. Reflect on these questions about that time in your life:

3. Going through this time of difficulty and cleansing, what challenges did I have to overcome?
   - Did I discover any hidden or unknown capacities I was carrying?
   - How and when did I feel cleansed or purified during this process?

4. Was there anyone or anything during this time that gave me a clearer sense of what was to come?
   - What was this vision of the future?

5. Did someone or something seem to tempt me, or distract me from my goal?
   - How did I handle this?

6. What has been my greatest sense of accomplishment during this renewal?
   - Did I find a new role, greater responsibility, or inner peace?
   - Did this include restoring a relationship with someone close to me?
   - Did I feel as though my inner potential was within reach?
   - What ideals, values, goals, or gifts did this experience confirm for me?

7. Write down your immediate thoughts to these questions in a rough outline, then transfer them to the appropriate archetype or motif on the following Purification worksheet. Later, transform these notes into a flowing narrative.

Workspace for Path of Purification Reflective Writing Exercise

_____

_____

_____

_____

_____

_____

_____

_____

_____

_____

_____

_____

_____

_____

Path of Purification Worksheet

ARCHETYPES & MOTIFS

Greater Challenges

Difficulties and trials; inner struggles; conflicts; sacrificing aspirations; suffering of any kind, such as an illness or loss, experiences of abuse; limitation of resources

Meaning

Discovering more of our innate ability; an opening up to whatever comes; purification of the self; need to be tempered

Personal Experience of the Archetype or Motif and its Personal Meaning

_____

_____

_____

_____

_____

Further Assistance

Meeting with a mentor; appearance of a guide; support from others; using inner resources; gaining a glimpse of the future

Meaning

Expansion of consciousness; movement toward the whole self; greater certainty of wholeness

Personal Experience of the Archetype or Motif and its Personal Meaning

_____

_____

_____

_____

_____

Temptation

Values tested; unethical conduct; substance abuse; compulsions; instant gratification

Meaning

Innocence transcended; personal standards challenged; ideals and values become confirmed; greater commitment to cleaning up and healing all parts of ourselves

Personal Experience of the Archetype or Motif and its Personal Meaning

_____

_____

_____

_____

_____

Renewal And Rebirth

Atonement; apotheosis; dying to the old, limited self; boon bestowed; peak experience; inner peace; taking control of our life; insight and change in therapy

Meaning

Letting go of old way of seeing things; some mysteries become clear; greater certainty of wholeness; fuller potential released; becoming more than we were; receipt of a gift to give back

Personal Experience of the Archetype or Motif and its Personal Meaning

_____

_____

_____

Path of Purification – Shaping a Narrative

From Notes to Narrative – Part II

After the first two Path of Purification exercises are completed to our satisfaction, we can take our notes from these and turn them into a flowing narrative telling our new story of greater challenges coming our way and transforming these into an opportunity for renewal.

This will most likely be a continuation of part one, although it could pick things up at a later point, too. We will probably see a common web of meaning linking the events of this phase to the events of the first part.

This muddle part of our journey reveals the inherent promise of our life, in which we find a new and more purposeful direction. In this portion, we resolve personal conflicts, and experience an important personal triumph, through an expansion of consciousness.

- Continuing on in the style used in the first part, focus on the difficulties, victories, and renewal just outlined on the worksheet, and turn these life experiences, and what they mean to you, into a clear, flowing story, being sure to express yourself with as much feeling as you possibly can.

- After completing a first draft, take enough time to really digest all the implications of this major change in your life before going on to the final part.

Return to Wholeness
Reflective Writing Exercise

Key Point

The current challenge is to integrate what we have been given into our own lives and give back or pass on our new understanding to others, while living in the wholeness we have discovered all around us. Finding a balance in our lives is necessary for maintaining the new perspective and understanding we've attained.

Writing Prompts

1. Use this as a mantra to meditate upon ~
   - *What we have been given is ours to give back.*

2. Thinking of those times in your life when you felt you had something to give others, and were able to do so, reflect on the following questions:

3. Were you ever reluctant, afraid, or unable to share an exhilarating experience with another?
   - Did it seem like you had something important to say but were prevented from communicating this?
   - Did you ever try to share something of real importance to you but have it misunderstood or disregarded?
   - How did you handle this disappointment?

4. Has offering someone something of importance to you ever helped maintain your self-assurance or commitment?

5. What was the boon, or gift, that you brought back for others?

6. Have you been able to accept your limitations and your achievements?

7. What has helped you remember that you are always in the process of becoming?

8. What is the one vision, dream, or goal that you live for?

9. Have you ever felt that your life is in harmony with some higher order?

10. What is the promise fulfilled of your life, or your contribution to the world?

11. What is the real meaning of the feelings you have just recalled?

12. Write down your rough thoughts, then transfer them to the following Return to Wholeness worksheet. Further reflect on what the three parts mean to you as a whole,

and then weave all three parts together into a complete flowing narrative of your entire consciousness journey.

Workspace for Return to Wholeness Reflective Writing Exercise

_____

_____

_____

_____

_____

_____

_____

_____

_____

_____

_____

_____

_____

_____

_____

Return to Wholeness Worksheet

ARCHETYPES & MOTIFS

Responsibility Accepted

Crossing the return threshold; initial feelings of insecurity or having enough support and resources to accomplish our task; obstacles don't prevent progress; surviving the impact; harsh realities handled; showing up for what is expected of us; giving back to others

Meaning

Test of commitment; return is supported; joys and sorrows accepted; self-assurance maintained

Personal Experience of the Archetype or Motif and its Personal Meaning

_____

_____

_____

_____

_____

Living In Wholeness

Master of two worlds; freedom to live consciously; doing what our roles call for; sharing a new message; success and failures accepted; content with our lot; serving the greater whole

Meaning

Living with a unitive consciousness; taking on a wider identity; living in balance and harmony; lifting up others; linking up with others; dedicated to the betterment of the world

Personal Experience of the Archetype or Motif and its Personal Meaning

_____

_____

_____

_____

_____

Return to Wholeness – Shaping and Merging the Narratives

From Notes to Narrative – Part III

After the first two Return to Wholeness exercises are completed to our satisfaction, we can begin to take our notes from these and turn them into a flowing narrative that tells our new story of focusing on sustaining the unitive consciousness we have come to be convinced of as the highest reality, while bringing back our boon to the world.

This conclusion of our journey to wholeness reveals the promise fulfilled of our life, when we are able to understand our role in and contribution to the world. Though this may be consciously understood, it may involve a long, even frustrating process of further adaptation and effort to achieve fully what we know is possible, but we have the assurance now that it is all worth the effort.

As we focus our thoughts on what we know has been a personal victory, we continue in the style of the first two parts to develop our personal experiences from the previous two exercises, and what they mean to us, into a well fleshed out story form that will become the conclusion of our journey to wholeness, a complete story, with a beginning, muddle, and resolution.

Merging the Three Parts of the Narrative into One Story

After completing this third part of the journey, we may want to reflect further on what the three parts mean to us as a whole. Considering them together, there may be some new insights that emerge as we reflect further on them in their entirety.

It may be that some new connections or hidden threads become clearer that were not apparent considering the parts by themselves. We may become aware of a previously unknown structure or pattern to our life which adds even more meaning to it.

This will be our final challenge in telling the story of our living into wholeness, to get as much meaning out of it as there is to be gotten.

As we see as much as there is to see in our overall experience of transformation and our return to wholeness, we will also understand that it is the very pattern that defines us that also has given us the most freedom in life to pursue the things that have most fulfilled us. We have gained a great appreciation of this ageless pattern, having lived it out in our own lives.

In reflecting further on the deeper, connective meaning in all three parts of this pattern as a whole, we have discovered through this process what Joseph Campbell called its ultimate aim, "neither release nor ecstasy for oneself, but the wisdom and the power to serve others," the essential message, or common truth, that the inner life of humanity has expressed forever.

Embracing every single element our experience has brought our way, all that has made us who we are, the sacrifices, the grace, the tests, the triumphs, our limits, and our expansiveness, we now take pleasure in merging all these parts into a greater whole, into the story of who we are at our essence, incorporating all the insights gained throughout this process making ours a new story for our time, to help lead us into the future long envisioned by our ancestors.

Meditation for Living into Wholeness

Find a quiet place,
get comfortable,
be still;
from your quiet mind,
breathe in…
breathe out…
Pause between each line.

In the beginning, there was wonderment...

In the beginning, there was contentment...

In the beginning, there was harmony...

In the beginning, there was peace...

In the beginning, there was wholeness...

Now, and for all time, may all beings live in wonderment...

Now, and for all time, may we all live in contentment...

Now, and for all time, may all beings live in harmony...

Now, and for all time, may we all live in peace...

Now, and for all time, may all beings live in wholeness...

In all our thoughts and actions,
    may we all remember to look upon all things with the eye of
    wholeness.

Acknowledgments

It takes a village to create a book. Many people have come together in this process to provide everything needed to take this from concept to manuscript to paperback.

I want to thank first my colleague and friend Kurt Johnson for encouraging me to pull together my life's work in a succinct and clear form. His ongoing support is deeply appreciated.

Since I have drawn from the best parts of many of my earlier books that all lead to this one, I want to thank again all those I have acknowledged in my previous books, too many to mention here individually, as this includes all my mentors, guides, and inspirations along the way, as well as the many students who have participated in workshops utilizing these tools for transformation.

I am extremely grateful to all the early readers of this manuscript, Lisa Worth Huber, Julie Krull, Jude Currivan, Jeff Vander Clute, Teresa Collins, Martha Schweitz, and Catherine Escamilla for their insights and encouragement when it was still in rough form.

The Light on Light Press team has been a pure delight to work with. I greatly value my collaboration with Kurt Johnson, Nomi Naeem, Karuna, and Sandra (Chamatkara) Simon, who have a wonderful thing going. It has also been great to work with Ariel Patricia and Sacred Stories Publishing a second time.

I am especially grateful to Jean Houston for her foreword and to Deepak Chopra for his afterword. They have both been very gracious in adding their wise words as valuable context in bringing greater clarity and relevance to this vital topic. I could not think of two better bookends for this synthesis of a lifetime of work.

Those invited to offer their advance thoughts on a book always have the tough job of reading something that hasn't yet seen the light of day and stake a lot on what they imagine it could become when it gets out there. For not only taking time out of their busy schedules to read this but also for taking a chance on its potential, I extend my deepest gratitude to those I have already mentioned and to Rev. Michael Bernard Beckwith, James O'Dea, Philip Goldberg, Steve Farrell, Shamini Jain, Anodea Judith, Lisa Engles Witter, and Michael Lindfield.

It has been a pleasure and a delight to work once again with Kate Sheehan Roach on this book. I am deeply grateful for her editorial skills and interspiritual eye, both of which have made crucial contributions to the book. She is gifted in knowing exactly what is needed, where to round everything out, and how to give the words their proper tone.

For his significant contribution to the book cover design, I am grateful to Brian Berman for the use of his unifying 9-spiral Holos sculpture, an inspired symbol representing wholeness, completeness, and one humanity. I also want to thank Elizabeth Campbell for her design of the consciousness continuum chart.

As always, my deepest appreciation and lasting gratitude goes to my first and most important reader, Cynthia Atkinson, who is always there with her honesty, understanding, and wisdom.

Notes

Preface

Plato, *The Republic*. Translated by F. M. Cornford. New York: Oxford University Press, 1951, 319.

The Hermetic Principle of the Law of Correspondence is one of seven Hermetic principles seen in nature and expressed in the Emerald Tablet and the Corpus Hermeticus from the teachings of Hermes Trismegistus, widely referred to in many spiritual traditions. https://en.wikipedia.org/wiki/Hermes_Trismegistus https://en.wiktionary.org/wiki/as_above,_so_below

unitive narrative https://www.evolutionaryleaders.net/unitivenarrative

Bahá'u'lláh, *Gleanings from the Writings of Bahá'u'lláh*. Wilmette, IL: Bahá'í Publishing Trust, 1976, 254.

Introduction

'Abdu'l-Bahá, *Some Answered Questions*. Wilmette, IL: Bahá'í Publishing Trust, 2014 ed., 199.

Pierre Teilhard de Chardin, *The Human Phenomenon*. Translated by Sarah Appleton-Weber. Portland, OR: Sussex Academic Press, 2003, 29.

Lao Tzu, *Tao Te Ching*. New York: HarperCollins, 2006, Ch. 1.

St. Catherine of Genoa, *Life and Doctrine of St. Catherine of Genoa*. Edited by Paul A. Boer Sr. Create Space: Veritas Splendor Publications, 2012, 227.

Joseph Campbell, *The Hero with a Thousand Faces*. New York: Meridian Books, 1949.

Arnold van Gennep, *The Rites of Passage*. Chicago: University of Chicago Press, 1960.

Evelyn Underhill, *Mysticism*. New York: Dutton, 1911/1961.

C.G. Jung, *Man and His Symbols*. New York: Random House, 2012, Part 3.

For more on *beginning, muddle, resolution*, see Robert Atkinson, *The Gift of Stories: Practical and Spiritual Applications of Autobiography, Life Stories, and Personal Mythmaking*. Westport, CT: Bergin and Garvey, 1995, 26, 30-32.

Tikkun Olam, https://www.myjewishlearning.com/article/tikkun-olam-repairing-the-world

'Abdu'l-Bahá, *Paris Talks*. London: Bahá'í Publishing Trust, 11th edition, 1969, 176-7.

C.G. Jung, *Psychological Reflections*. Princeton: Princeton University Press, 1973.

C.G. Jung, *The Spirit in Man, Art and Literature*. Princeton: Princeton University Press, 1971.

Joseph Campbell, *The Masks of God. Vol. 4, Creative Mythology.* New York: Viking, 1970; *Myths to Live By.* New York: Viking, 1972.

Chapter 1

Bede Griffiths, *A New Vision of Reality: Western Science, Eastern Mysticism and Christian Faith.* Springfield. IL: Templegate Publishers, 1990.

Charles Darwin, *The Descent of Man.* New York: Penguin Classics, 2004, 147.

Ken Wilber, *The Marriage of Sense and Soul.* New York: Broadway Books, 1998, Ch. 8.

Guy Gugliotta, "The Great Human Migration," *Smithsonian Magazine*, July, 2008. https://www.smithsonianmag.com/history/the-great-human-migration-13561/

David Sloan Wilson, *This View of Life: Completing the Darwinian Revolution.* New York: Vintage, 2019.

'Abdu'l-Bahá, *Some Answered Questions.* Wilmette, IL: Bahá'í Publishing Trust, 1987, 198-9.

Paul Carus, *The Gospel of Buddha.* Chicago: Open Court Publishing, 1915, 142.

Ethen Siegal, "What is the Most Astounding Fact About the Universe?" in *Forbes/Science*, April, 2016.

Ervin Laszlo, *The Inner Limits of Mankind: Heretical Reflections on Today's Values, Culture and Politics.* Oxford: Oneworld Publications, 1989, 65-7, 120-28.

Hans Kung, editor, *A Global Ethic: The Declaration of the Parliament of World Religions*. New York: Continuum, 1993, 34-5.

Chapter 2

Evelyn Underhill, *Mysticism*, 445.

Elizabeth Gilbert, *Eat, Pray, Love*. New York: Penguin, 2007, 154.

C.G. Jung, *Psychological Reflections*, ibid, 22, 29-31.

'Abdu'l-Bahá, *The Promulgation of Universal Peace*. Wilmette, IL: Bahá'í Publishing Trust, 1982, 152.

'Abdu'l-Bahá, *Some Answered Questions*, ibid, 210.

C.G. Jung, *Memories, Dreams, Reflections*. New York: Vintage, 1963, 3-5.

C.G. Jung, *Psychological Reflections*, ibid, 172.

Chapter 3

Johanna Macy, quoted in Marilyn Schlitz and Tina Amorok, *Consciousness and Healing: Integral Approaches to Mind-Body Medicine*. London: Churchill Livingstone, 2004, 530.

Bahá'í writings: Universal House of Justice, *The Promise of World Peace*. October 1985.
https://www.bahai.org/library/authoritative-texts/the-universal-house-of-justice/messages/19851001_001/19851001_001.pdf

C.G. Jung, *Memories, Dreams, Reflections*. New York: Vintage, 1963, 311, 335, 345.

Jolande Jacobi, *The Psychology of C.G. Jung*. New Haven: Yale University Press, 1973, 53-55.

Heraclitus, https://en.wikipedia.org/wiki/Heraclitus#Unity_of_opposites

C.G. Jung, *Collected Works of C.G. Jung, V.12*. Princeton: Princeton University Press, 1980, 6.

Desmond Tutu and Mpho Tutu, *Made for Goodness*. New York: Harper One, 2010, 7.

Ervin Laszlo, *Worldshift 2012*. Rochester, VT: Inner Traditions, 2009, Ch. 1, 99, 111.

Chapter 4

C. G. Jung, *Modern Man in Search of a Soul*. New York: Harcourt, 1933, 211, 217.

Anodea Judith, *The Global Heart Awakens*. San Rafael, CA: Shift Books, 2013, 42.

Twelve Steps https://en.wikipedia.org/wiki/Twelve-step_program

Joseph Campbell, *The Hero with a Thousand Faces*. New York: Meridian Books, 1949, 3.

St. Augustine quoted in Evelyn Underhill, *Mysticism*, ibid, 178.

Bahá'u'lláh, *The Seven Valleys and the Four Valleys*. Wilmette, IL: Bahá'í Publishing Trust, 1973.

Rumi, *Love is a Stranger: Selected Lyric Poetry of Jalal al-Din Rumi*. Translated by Kabir Helminski. Boston: Shambhala, 2000.

Joni Mitchell, "Urge for Going." https://www.youtube.com/watch?v=SlrWjxwZTpQ

Arlo Guthrie, "Highway in the Wind." https://www.youtube.com/watch?v=-SyofNCVXSs

Cat Stevens, "Miles from Nowhere." https://www.youtube.com/watch?v=fsI5IiHVVXw

Carole King, "Way Over Yonder." https://www.youtube.com/watch?v=G8se6T5d3K0

Moody Blues, "Dawning Is the Day." https://www.youtube.com/watch?v=ueYhXHBIORA

Joseph Campbell, *The Hero with a Thousand Faces*, ibid, 25.

Chapter 5

Marion Woodman, in Nancy Ryley, *The Forsaken Garden: Four Conversations on the Deep Meaning of Environmental Illness*. Wheaton, IL: Quest Books, 1998, 120.

C.G. Jung, *Collected Works*, Vol.12, 6.

Joseph Campbell, *The Hero with a Thousand Faces*, ibid, ch. II.

John Welwood, https://www.johnwelwood.com/articles/TRIC_interview_uncut.pdf

Suso, quoted in Evelyn Underhill, *Mysticism*, ibid.

Merswin, quoted in Evelyn Underhill, *Mysticism*, ibid.

Bahá'u'lláh, *The Seven Valleys*, ibid.

Laura Nyro, "Time and Love." https://www.youtube.com/watch?v=3_69YAIa2CE

Bob Dylan, "Girl from the North Country." https://www.youtube.com/watch?v=tMNOuJ977I0

James Taylor, "Something in the Way She Moves." https://www.youtube.com/watch?v=YoevtZiVR4k

Carole King, "Tapestry." https://www.youtube.com/watch?v=SAqYzqHdXu8

Chapter 6

Bahá'u'lláh, *Gleanings* ibid, 184.

Desmond Tutu and Mpho Tutu, *Made for Goodness*, ibid, x, 5, 43.

Thomas Merton, "Hagia Sophia," in Thomas P. McDonnell, ed. *A Thomas Merton Reader*. New York: Doubleday, 1974, 506.

Evelyn Underhill, *Mysticism*, ibid, 437.

Bahá'u'lláh, *The Seven Valleys*, ibid, 17-29.

Moody Blues, "Balance." https://www.youtube.com/watch?v=bA9A9a5A090

Bob Dylan, "New Morning." https://www.youtube.com/watch?v=99s-B9YoGPA

Joni Mitchell, "Circle Game." https://www.youtube.com/watch?v=f_eMZsxmNnk

Cat Stevens, "Morning Has Broken." https://www.youtube.com/watch?v=3Rifby1tVE8

Carole King, "Beautiful."
https://www.youtube.com/watch?v=vIBhzZxy3bs

John Lennon, "Imagine."
https://www.youtube.com/watch?v=pfcJ9_C6SOM

Epilogue

Elisabet Sahtouris, "Letter for the Future," in *Our Moment of Choice. Evolutionary Visions and Hope for the Future*, edited by Robert Atkinson, Kurt Johnson, and Deborah Moldow. New York: Atria, 2020, 287-292.

Joseph Campbell with Bill Moyers, *The Power of Myth*. New York, 1991, 41.

Ervin Laszlo, "Reasoning and Experiencing Our Way to Oneness," *Our Moment of Choice*, ibid, 273-8.

Michael Bernard Beckwith, "Is World Peace Possible?" in *Our Moment of Choice*, ibid, 33-38.

James O'Dea, "The Great Map of Peace," in *Our Moment of Choice*, ibid, 3-10.

Universal House of Justice, *The Promise of World Peace*, ibid.

Universal House of Justice, *To the Baha'is of the United States*, July 22, 2020.
https://www.bahai.org/library/authoritative-texts/the-universal-house-of-justice/messages/20200722_001/1#870410250

Further Resources

Robert Atkinson, Kurt Johnson, and Deborah Moldow (editors) *Our Moment of Choic e: Evolutionary Visions and Hope for the Future*. New York: Atria/Beyond Words, 2020).

A timely, compelling, and comprehensive anthology of essential essays by 43 Evolutionary Leaders offering creative and practical solutions to the many crises facing humanity as a call-to-action for transforming the world into a just, peaceful, and thriving whole in which all components are linked as one.

Robert Atkinson, *The Story of Our Time: From Duality to Interconnectedness to Oneness* (Delray Beach, FL: Sacred Stories Publishing, 2017).

A deeply thoughtful narrative of the evolution of consciousness framed by seven unifying principles drawn from the world's wisdom traditions that illustrate a purposeful direction to social evolution toward a unitive consciousness providing the context, framework, and vision for humanity's next step in its evolution.

Robert Atkinson, *Year of Living Deeply: A Memoir of 1969* (Wilmette, IL: One Voice Press, 2019).

> A soulful, meditative memoir reflecting on the hidden meanings of a series of transformative experiences, adventures, and events coinciding with a year that shaped a generation and highlighting a timeless, universal pattern that links this personal story to the stories of countless others.

Robert Atkinson, *Mystic Journey: Getting to the Heart of Your Soul's Story* (New York: Cosimo Books, 2012).

> A guide to soul-making, or living our lives consciously, from the world's mystic traditions that reveals a practice for remembering who we are and defines a universal, all-human path lined with motifs and archetypes making up a pattern connecting us to all others and leading us toward personal and collective transformation while living with an eternal perspective on life.

Robert Atkinson, *The Gift of Stories: Practical and Spiritual Applications of Autobiography, Life Stories, and Personal Mythmaking* (Westport, CT: Praeger, 1995).

> An exploration of the timeless power of traditional and sacred stories that are designed to connect, transform, and unite both tellers and listeners in ever expanding circles, as well as a guide to writing and telling one's own story within a pattern framed by universal motifs and archetypes that shape and deeply change our lives.

Joseph Campbell, *The Hero with a Thousand Faces* (Princeton: Princeton University Press, 1973).

> The classic, best-selling exploration of world mythology that identifies the pattern of the monomyth, or journey of the hero, and the timeless, universal motifs and archetypes that transform our lives as well.

Evelyn Underhill, *Mysticism: A Study of the Nature and Development of Man's Spiritual Consciousness* (New York: Dutton, 1961).

> Originally published in 1901, the classic work of mysticism drawing upon the lived experience of the great mystics, women and men, illuminating the path of the mystic way and detailing the process of awakening, purification, the dark night of the soul, and union.

Bahá'u'lláh, *The Seven Valleys* in *Call of the Divine Beloved: Selected Mystical Works of Bahá'u'lláh* (Haifa: Bahá'í World Centre, 2018).

> *The Seven Valleys*, written by Bahá'u'lláh in 1856, was addressed to Sufi mystics familiar with *The Conference of the Birds*, a 12th century poem by Attar taking its title from the Qur'an and using the journey of the birds to their source as a metaphor for humans and humanity as a whole. *The Seven Valleys* expands upon this and reveals the mysteries of the evolutionary stages of the soul's ascent in its journey to wholeness.

Index

Y

About the Author

Robert Atkinson, PhD, award-winning author, educator, and developmental psychologist, is a 2020 Gold Nautilus Book Award winner as co-editor of *Our Moment of Choice: Evolutionary Visions and Hope for the Future*, and a 2017 Silver Nautilus Book Award winner for *The Story of Our Time: From Duality to Interconnectedness to Oneness*. He is also the author or co-editor of eight other books including *Year of Living Deeply: A Memoir of 1969* (2019), *Mystic Journey: Getting to the Heart of Your Soul's Story* (2012), and *The Gift of Stories* (1995).

With a PhD in cross-cultural human development from the University of Pennsylvania and a postdoctoral fellowship at the University of Chicago, he is professor emeritus at the University of Southern Maine, an internationally recognized authority on life story interviewing, a pioneer in the techniques of personal myth-making and soul-making, director of StoryCommons, founder of One Planet Peace Forum, and a member of the Evolutionary Leaders. www.robertatkinson.net